S0-GIB-416

THE CRIMINALITY

OF

WOMEN

By

OTTO POLLAK

DISCARD

A Perpetua Book

A. S. Barnes & Company, Inc.

New York

Andrew S. Thomas Memorial Library
MORRIS HARVEY COLLEGE, CHARLESTON, W. VA:

46530

364.37
P76c

Copyright 1950

UNIVERSITY OF PENNSYLVANIA PRESS

Manufactured in the United States of America

PERPETUA EDITION 1961

To G. K. P.

ACKNOWLEDGMENTS

Too numerous to mention them all are those who have helped the author in his work on this study. The outstanding character of their assistance makes it his pleasant duty, however, to express his special gratitude to the following persons. First of all, the writer is indebted to Dr. Thorsten Sellin and Dr. J. P. Shalloo of the University of Pennsylvania. Dr. Sellin suggested this undertaking and guided it with the discerning and incisive counsel for which he is known through its various stages until his departure for Sweden in 1946 prevented his seeing it through to its end. Dr. Shalloo, having also assisted the author's work from the beginning, is largely responsible for the crystallization of the writer's thoughts and for the organization of the material in its final form. Special thanks are further due to Dr. Ernest W. Burgess of the University of Chicago, under whose guidance an exploratory study of some aspects of the criminality of women was undertaken.

For valuable assistance the author is also indebted to Miss Mary M. Zender, Lecturer in Social Case Work at Bryn Mawr College, and to Dr. Harry Helson, Chairman of the Department of Psychology at Brooklyn College. Miss Zender submitted with endless patience to the writer's request for the reactions of a woman scientist to his findings and made many valuable suggestions. With equal kindness, Dr. Helson guided the writer to psychological source material and gave the necessary reactions from the angle of his science. For consultation on legal questions, the author takes pleasure in acknowledging his debt to Mr. Frederick W. Killian, member of the New York Bar and Associate Professor of Sociology at Clark University. He owes further a special debt of appreciation to all the members of the Department of Sociology at the University of Pennsylvania, who over a period of years had to listen to his scientific concerns in the process of his study and have unfailingly and invariably shown the interest and forbearance which become scholars and gentlemen.

The author feels that this list of acknowledgments must not come to an end without the expression of his awareness of the great services rendered him by the librarians Mr. Elliott H. Morse and Misses Flora Deibert, Dorothea Manning, and Elizabeth Thorp of the University of Pennsylvania; Miss Lois Antoinette Reed, Mrs. Marie Good Hunt, and Miss Mary Louise Terrien of Bryn Mawr College; and Dr. W. B. McDaniel II, Miss Clara Manson, Mrs. M. G. Maines, and Miss Anna Ludovici of the College of Physicians, Philadelphia. All of them have shown the writer a degree of helpfulness in the unearthing of out-of-the-way books for which he can hardly be grateful enough.

Sincere appreciation is due to the Social Science Research Council which, at first with a fellowship and at a later stage with a demobilization award, has assisted the writer in his work on this study.

O. P.

University of Pennsylvania

CONTENTS

TABLES

INTRODUCTION

The criminality of women is a neglected field of research. Our mental picture of the criminal is that of a male violator of the law, and criminological research seems to have been largely under the spell of this cultural stereotype. The lack of scientific attention to the problems presented by women offenders is probably due to the ever recurrent observation that considerably smaller numbers of women come into contact with the law-enforcing agencies than do men.[1] Women, however, represent about half of our population and live under conditions which may often protect them against the detection or prosecution of crime. These conditions suggest that female criminality deserves more research interest than it has received, no matter how small its numerical importance may appear on the basis of criminal statistics taken at their face value.

Within recent years various scholars have drawn attention to this neglect of the study of the criminality of women. Thorsten Sellin and Walter C. Reckless did so in two research memoranda published by the Social Science Research Council, T. E. Sullenger in an article in the *Journal of Criminal Law and Criminology*, and Harry Elmer Barnes and Negley K. Teeters in their book on *New Horizons in Criminology*.[2] These research suggestions will probably be taken up in the near future, and it is the purpose of this study to assist in such endeavors by presenting an integrated analysis of the major conjectures and research findings so far available in the American, English, French, and German literature. Some references will also be made to Italian, Dutch, and South American material, but source material from these countries is not presented with any claim to coverage because of the limited language competence of the writer, which prevented his ready access to these sources.

The nature of the problem of female criminality has been differently conceived by the authors who have paid attention to it so far. Comparatively great interest seems to have been elicited by the quantitative aspect of the problem. A number of writers have focused their interest on the apparent disproportion between male and female offenders and have tried to explain this phenomenon in various ways. A majority of them have fully, or at least partially, accepted the impression furnished by criminal statistics and have concluded that women are less criminal than men. They believe in the existence of a numerical differential but vary in their interpretation of its causes. Some of these writers believe in an inherent sex differential regarding conformity. Others refer to social conditions and particularly to the narrower sphere of activities open to women as the reason for the differential. Those using the latter interpretation expect an increase in the criminality of women as a concomitant of their success in achieving social equality with men. Both opinions have been expressed fairly early in the history of criminology and both still seem to find adherents.

In the first group belongs Louis Proal, who in 1892 declared that the criminality of men was so much greater than that of women that it was impossible not to admit the moral superiority of women over men.[3] Exactly fifty years later, a South American writer, J. Belby, seems to have voiced a similar opinion by proposing the thesis that in all cultures and societies woman is rarely criminal and that the few exceptions to this rule are due to the development of masculine traits.[4] In this country, Amram Scheinfeld has recently expressed the belief that the female sex is for biological reasons more submissive than the male and that the numerical sex differential in criminal behavior is neither environmentally caused nor illusory.[5]

Between those who believe in an inherent sex differential in crime and those who consider it as socially caused and therefore subject to change stand a few who explain the apparent numerical disproportion between male and female offenders by an interplay of biological and social factors. Representatives of this group are Luke Owen Pike, Georg Buschan, Pauline Tarnowsky, and Johanna C. Hudig. The historical nature of Pike's study made him aware of the impact of social conditioning without, however, blinding him to the biological basis of human behavior.

This synthetic point of view led him to explain the apparent numerical sex differential in crime by the social aftereffects of earlier periods, in which physical strength may have been more necessary for criminal acts than in his day. According to him, the lesser strength of woman's body prevented her from becoming as criminal as man in cruder periods of time, and the habits of behavior so formed persisted into the nineteenth century, as reflected in the criminal statistics of his time. He pointed out, however, that the prevalence of town life and the increasing independence of women were changing the old patterns of behavior and causing an increase in female crime.[6]

Georg Buschan's main interest in his study of sex and crime was that of a physician who emphasized biological and physiological factors, but he was aware of social implications and explained the numerical sex differential as being the result of the interaction of biological and social conditions.[7] Pauline Tarnowsky similarly believed in a quantitative sex differential in crime and thought the lower incidence of women among murderers due to biological and social influences.[8] Johanna C. Hudig, a recent writer on the subject, believes that the factors of biological disposition and environment in their interaction produce in women a greater degree of adaptability than they produce in men. According to her, this differential in adaptability accounts for the quantitative sex differential between male and female crime.[9]

Those scholars who reject any biological explanation and explain the numerical sex differential purely in terms of social conditions are more numerous. In the United States, it was interestingly enough a physician, Ely van de Warker, who as early as 1875 took a stand against the belief in an inherent higher morality of the female sex and pointed to woman's lack of opportunity, the nature of her occupations, and her comparative protection against temptation as an explanation of her lower participation in crime.[10] An explanation along the same lines was offered by Clarence Darrow in 1922[11] and repeated by Sullenger in 1936 in his analysis of female criminality in Omaha.[12] In Italy, Napoleone Colajanni in 1889 and Dora Melegari in 1903 took similar positions, rejecting the idea of higher female morality and explaining the numerical sex differential in terms of social conditions.

Colajanni envisaged a future in which sex equality would be reached and consequently both sexes would participate equally in crime.[13] In the Netherlands, Cornelis Loosjes proposed the same thesis in 1894 and tried to support it by showing that the criminality figures of women in the various European countries seemed to be correlated with the relative approach of women to social equality with men, the figures being lowest in the Eastern, highest in the Western, and somewhat in between in the Central European countries.[14] Woman's lack of opportunity and supposedly fewer temptations to commit crimes were again pointed out in 1912 by the French writer Jean Finot, and recent reiterations of the same basic theory have come in 1937 from the Belgian scholar Etienne de Greeff and the Polish criminologist L. Radzinowicz.[15]

The acceptance of the numerical sex differential in criminal statistics, however, met challengers. In 1910, H. Leale, a Swiss author, published a penetrating analysis of the various inadequacies of criminal statistics in measuring female offenses and came to the conclusion that in all probability both sexes participated equally in crime. Others, among them Frances A. Kellor, William A. Bonger, Clarence Darrow, Maurice Parmelee, Johanna C. Hudig, Arthur Evans Wood, and John Barker Waite, have also expressed the contention that criminal statistics do not measure male and female crime to the same degree, without, however, reaching Leale's radical conclusion.[16]

Another group of authors such as Hans Gross, Karl Birnbaum, and Friedrich Leppmann has been more interested in the qualitative aspect of the criminality of women and has stressed the differences between male and female psychology as well as the influence of woman's developmental phases upon the etiology of female crime. According to these writers, the crux of the problem is not to be found in the quantitative but in the qualitative differences between the criminal behavior patterns of the two sexes and in differences in the causative factors related to these different types of behavior.[17]

Lombroso combined the quantitative and the qualitative approach, and explained the apparently lower participation of women in crime by a lower degree of variability in the physical, physiological, and sensory character of women. However, he considered prostitution as the female equivalent of criminality in the male, and on that basis concluded that the similarity in extent of male and female nonconformity is greater than usually believed.[18] In recent years, Alfredo Niceforo has reiterated the Lombrosian position regarding the balancing effect of prostitution in this respect.[19]

There is finally a group of investigators who have concentrated on the study of certain characteristics of the female offender. The American authors in this group have been particularly interested in questions of health, intelligence, exposure to economic pressure, and unfavorable home environment. This line of investigation was started in the second decade of the twentieth century and has persisted up to the present time. It is represented by Edith Abbott, Augusta F. Bronner, Edith R. Spaulding, Alberta S. B. Guibord, Mabel Ruth Fernald, Sheldon Glueck, Eleanor T. Glueck, and others.[20] European writers who have been interested in this line of research have concentrated on studying the age factor and the marital status of the offender in female crime. The work of Friedrich Prinzing, Hugo Hoegel, and Hans Krille deserves attention in this respect.[21]

Most of the authors mentioned in this chapter have made important contributions to our knowledge of the criminality of women, but their particularistic approach has prevented them from giving an integrated picture of the phenomenon of female crime and has led to a neglect of some characteristic aspects of female criminality by all of them.

The approach selected by this writer is that of a study of the criminality of a population group as suggested by Thorsten Sellin in his *War and Crime: A Research Memorandum*.[22] Such an approach seems to require the investigation of at least the following aspects of the phenomenon: (1) the ways in which women commit their crimes, (2) the amount of female criminality with consideration, not only of the apparent, but also of all indications regarding the real criminality of women, (3) the specificity of female crime, (4) the personal characteristics of female offenders, and (5) the factors of causation which distinguish women criminals from other offender groups. This ap-

...oach has made it necessary for the writer to draw upon a wide range of sources. As already indicated, sufficient material on women offenders is not contained in publications directly and primarily concerned with female criminality as such. A wealth of information, however, can be gained from criminological sources devoted to other subjects but mentioning the one or the other aspect of female criminality as an aside or for purposes of illustration. Much material is also available in medical literature, and additional information can be derived from publications in such varied fields as biographies of detectives and criminals, psychological research, and the discussion of specific crime damages in trade journals. By using all these types of material within the common frame of reference of female criminality, it is hoped to avoid the dangers of selective consideration of the female factor in crime from one or a few specific angles of research interest which has characterized the pertinent literature in the past.

NOTES

For full identification of the works quoted in the Notes following this Introduction and all Chapters, see Bibliography.

[1] Fred E. Haynes, *Criminology*, 2nd ed., p. 328; Donald Reed Taft, *Criminology*, p. 75; Walter C. Reckless, *Criminal Behavior*, p. 96; Edwin H. Sutherland, *Principles of Criminology*, 3rd ed., pp. 99-100; and many others.

[2] Thorsten Sellin, *War and Crime: A Research Memorandum*, p. 10; Walter C. Reckless, *The Etiology of Delinquent and Criminal Behavior*, pp. 88, 90; T. E. Sullenger, "Female Criminality in Omaha," *Journal of Criminal Law and Criminology*, XXVII (1936-37), 711; Harry Elmer Barnes and Negley K. Teeters, *New Horizons in Criminology*, p. 572.

[3] Louis Proal, *Le Crime et la Peine*, p. 61.

[4] J. Belby, "Female Delinquency," *Arch. Med. leg. Argent.*, XII (1942), 3-20.

[5] Amram Scheinfeld, *Women and Men*, p. 244.

[6] Luke Owen Pike, *A History of Crime in England*, II, p. 527.

[7] Georg Buschan, *Geschlecht und Verbrechen*, 3rd ed., p. 37.

[8] Pauline Tarnowsky, *Les Femmes Homicides*, pp. 95, 101 ff.

[9] Johanna C. Hudig, *De Criminaliteit Der Vrouw*, pp. 255-58.

[10] Ely van de Warker, "The Relations of Women to Crime," *The Popular Science Monthly*, VIII (1875-76), 5.

[11] Clarence Darrow, *Crime, Its Causes and Treatment*, p. 72.

[12] Sullenger, *op. cit.*, p. 706.

[13] Napoleone Colajanni, *La Sociologia Criminale*, II, pp. 91 ff.; Dora Melegari, "La Femme Criminelle en Italie," *Le Correspondant*, CCX (1903), 532.

[14] Cornelis Loosjes, *Bijdrage Tot De Studie Van De Criminaliteit Der Vrouw*, p. 61.

15 Jean Finot, *Préjugé et Problème des Sexes*, p. 301; Etienne de Greeff, *Introduction à la Criminologie*, p. 103; L. Radzinowicz, "Variability of the Sex-Ratio of Criminality," *The Sociological Review*, XXIX (1937), 76-102.

16 H. Leale, "De la Criminalité des Sexes," *Archives D'Anthropologie Criminelle*, XXV (1910), 415, 421; Frances A. Kellor, *Experimental Sociology*, p. 159; William A. Bonger, *Criminality and Economic Conditions*, p. 472; Darrow, *op. cit.*, p. 72; Maurice Parmelee, *Criminology*, pp. 245-46; Arthur Evans Wood and John Barker Waite, *Crime and Its Treatment*, p. 238; Hudig, *op. cit.*, p. 255.

17 Hans Gross, *Kriminalpsychologie*, 2nd ed., p. 474; Karl Birnbaum, *Die Psychopathischen Verbrecher*, p. 318; Friedrich Leppmann, "Weibliche Generationsphasen und Kriminalität," *Archiv für Frauenkunde und Konstitutionsforschung*, XIV (1928), 292-321.

18 Cesare Lombroso, *Crime: Its Causes and Remedies*, p. 185; Gina Lombroso Ferrero, *Criminal Man*, pp. 292 ff; Cesare Lombroso and Guglielmo Ferrero, *Das Weib als Verbrecherin und Prostituierte*, p. vi. The German translation is preferable to the English translation because the latter does not cover the whole work and has appeared only in 1,000 copies, which are hard to locate.

19 Alfredo Niceforo, *Criminologia ** Ambiente e Delinquenza*, p. 709.

20 Edith R. Spaulding, "The Results of Mental and Physical Examinations of Four Hundred Women Offenders—With Particular Reference to Their Treatment During Commitment," *Journal of the American Institute of Criminal Law and Criminology*, V (1914-15), 704-17; Alberta S. B. Guibord, "Physical States of Criminal Women," *ibid.*, VIII (1917-18), 82-95; Augusta F. Bronner, *A Comparative Study of the Intelligence of Delinquent Girls;* Mabel Ruth Fernald *et al., A Study of Women Delinquents in New York State;* Mary Jean Bowman, "Economic Aspects of the Histories of Reformatory Women"; Sophonisba Preston Breckinridge and Edith Abbott, *The Delinquent Child and the Home;* Sheldon and Eleanor T. Glueck, *Five Hundred Delinquent Women.*

21 Friedrich Prinzing, "Die Erhöhung der Kriminalität des Weibes durch die Ehe," *Zeitschrift für Sozialwissenschaft*, II, Alte Folge (1899), 433-50; Hugo Hoegel, "Die Straffälligkeit des Weibes," *Archiv für Kriminal-Anthropologie*, V (1900), 231-89; Hans Krille, *Weibliche Kriminalität und Ehe.*

22 Sellin, *War and Crime: A Research Memorandum*, p. 10.

CHAPTER I

THE MASKED CHARACTER OF FEMALE CRIME

Women have received more commendations for their seemingly low criminality than practically any other population group. As already pointed out, however, these favorable statements have not gone unchallenged. The relationships between the real, the apparent, and the legal criminality of women therefore need a special investigation. In this respect, three questions suggest themselves to the student of criminal statistics: (1) Are those crimes in which women seem to participate exclusively, or to a considerable extent, offenses which are known to be greatly underreported? (2) Are women offenders generally less often detected than are men offenders? (3) Do women, if apprehended, meet with more leniency than do men? It seems that each of these three questions will have to be answered in the affirmative and that the long discussion which has centered around the apparent numerical sex differential in crime may have been based on a statistical deception.

An investigation of the first question shows that some offenses which are frequently committed by women are greatly underreported. Shoplifting of nonprofessional character, thefts by prostitutes, domestic thefts, abortions, perjury, and disturbance of the peace have to be primarily considered in this respect. These are crimes which are very unsatisfactorily reflected in criminal statistics[1] and, at the same time, are offenses in which women take an outstanding or even an exclusive part. Woman the shopper is also the representative shoplifter. Woman the mother is also the abortee. The prostitute living on the fringes of society with many contacts among criminals is one of the least prosecuted thieves in our society because of the obvious non-

1

coöperation of the victim with the police. For reasons which will be indicated later, woman is frequently a perjurer; and because of her irritability at certain times she is often also a disturber of the peace. It seems, therefore, that Lombroso and Paul Pollitz were justified in their statements that the crimes to which women are particularly addicted are those which are most easily concealed and which most rarely lead to trial.[2]

Then there are also offenses which, although prosecuted in cases of male offenders, remain practically unprosecuted if committed by women. Homosexual contacts between women are hardly ever apprehended, but are by no means so infrequent as is often assumed.[3] How practically untouched this type of offense is by criminal prosecution, if it is committed by women, can be gathered from the fact that in the ten-year period 1930-40 only two adult women were prosecuted and convicted on charges of Lesbianism in New York.[4] Of the 2,022 cases of sex offenders covered by the study of the Mayor's Committee in New York, only one sodomy case involved women alone.[5]

Exhibitionism occurs frequently among girls. This can be easily observed by anyone who passes the streets with open eyes to human behavior, but no prosecution on that charge has been recorded.[6] Similarly, being an accessory to statutory rape is hardly ever charged to a woman. Again, only one such case was found among the 2,022 sex offenders investigated by the Mayor's Committee in New York.[7] Still, we can have little doubt that at least women who keep houses of ill fame must commit this offense as accessories[8] repeatedly in the course of their work.

Factors of a more general nature than the type of the offense as such contribute also to a great divergence between the real and the apparent criminality of women. It is part of our culture that women should be protected by men. The strength of this conventional norm also affects our struggle with female crime. Male victims of female offenders are less inclined to bring complaint to the authorities than the victims of male criminals.[9]

Another cultural factor closely related to our male attitude of protectiveness works similarly against the detectability of female crime. Our culture imposed until very recently, and partly still imposes, a comparatively inactive role upon women. The lack of social equality between the sexes has led to a cultural distribution of roles which forces women in many cases into the part of the instigator rather than of the performer of an overt act. It is customary in our society that man should assume the active role in many spheres of life. This cultural arrangement finds its expression also in crime, and several authors have drawn attention to the observation that women participate in crime often as accomplices rather than as independent perpetrators. Women have been said to be the criminal "powers behind the throne," to furnish the brains in many a predatory crime, and actually to perform almost every part in the commission of certain gang crimes except that of the actual perpetration.[10] The fact that accomplices and especially instigators are harder to detect or to prosecute successfully than overt perpetrators must help many women offenders to escape punishment[11] and must adversely affect the value of criminal statistics with regard to female crime.

Very important in this respect is the specific method of procedure which distinguishes female from male offenders. This is an aspect of female criminality which has to be considered in many respects for an understanding of the whole phenomenon and will be fully discussed in later chapters. Suffice it to mention here that many crimes which are considered highly detectable lose this quality when they are committed by women because of the way in which they are carried out. The division of labor in our society assigns to women the roles of the homemaker, the rearer of children, the nurse of the sick, the domestic helper, and the passive partner in emotional relationships. It furnishes them thereby many opportunities to commit crimes in ways and by means which are not available to men and which reduce the public character of many offenses. In order to avoid undue repetition of material which will be presented later, only one example will be given here for purposes of illustration. Murder is considered as a crime of highly public character. If committed by women, however, this crime may not be so highly detectable because female murderers resort to poison to a much higher degree than men.[12]

Finally, we have to consider the phenomenon of greater leniency for women who come into contact with our machinery of law enforcement. Except in times of aroused public opinion, our police are inclined to treat unofficially all minor offenses of young girls in order to save them from the social stigma which follows an appearance in court.[13] Patrolmen and male detectives do not like to arrest women,[14] because these officers are frequently confused by the apparent violation of our norms of behavior between men and women which such a professional act on their part seems to imply. Women police officials, however, are mostly assigned to special work with juveniles and are seldom employed in general apprehension and detection work. Prosecutors are apprehensive of the difficulties in achieving the conviction of a woman who is free from earlier social stigma, and sometimes are even apologetic in the performance of their official duties regarding female offenders.

From many quarters have come complaints about an acquittal bias on the part of judges and juries in women's cases.[15] Most people who follow trials in this and other countries will recall instances in which traditional chivalry in the courtroom and the conventional prejudices of public opinion have led to acquittals which were by no means in accordance with the evidence, but reflected our cultural attitudes toward women.

Statistics seem to corroborate largely the so frequently stated impression that misplaced gallantry interferes with convictions of

TABLE 1
CONVICTIONS RESULTING FROM ARRESTS FOR MAJOR CRIMES, BY SEX, NEW YORK STATE, 1940*

Type of Crime	Percentage of Arrests	
	Male	Female
Homicide	25	33
Robbery	40	17
Assault	15	6
Burglary	26	20
Larceny, Grand	40	28
Auto theft	21	15
Receiver of stolen property	20	9
Forgery	38	25

* Based on Marie E. Costello, "Some Indications of Trend in Female Criminality in the United States," unpublished manuscript. The percentages worked up by Miss Costello are based on absolute arrest and conviction figures contained in State of New York, *Eleventh Annual Report of the Commissioner of Correction on Crime Statistics*, pp. 414, 420.

women offenders. Of 20,000 men arrested in New York State in 1940, 57 per cent were convicted; of the little over 1,000 women arrested in the same year, only 43 per cent were convicted.[16] A breakdown by major offenses shows a similar picture except for homicide, for which the relationship seems reversed (Table 1).

The gallantry of the French juries is notorious and finds its expression in the following figures.

TABLE 2

ACQUITTALS OF THE FRENCH ASSIZES, ACCORDING TO SEX OF THE DEFENDANT*

| Period | Number of Acquitted per 100 Indicted Persons of the Same Sex | |
	Male	Female
1856-60	23	33
1876-80	19	35
1888-92	23.4	47.8

* Based on Hoegel, *op. cit.*, p. 235.

A few figures from Chicago seem to offer some statistical counter-evidence but on closer analysis resolve into a confirmation of the observation that our courts treat women more leniently than they treat men. According to the report of the City Council Committee on Crime of the City of Chicago, only 44.8 per cent of the 97,393 male arrests studied led to convictions, while 48.1 per cent of the 12,371 female arrests ended in convictions. The report points out, however, that the convicted women were more frequently fined than the men and that convictions of women were more easily secured for this reason.[17] It therefore must be concluded that, at least in many instances, police, prosecution, and courts are biased in favor of women offenders and that criminal statistics must be analyzed with corresponding caution.

All these considerations suggest strongly that the criminality of women is largely masked criminality. In order to avoid a misinterpretation of the sex differential apparent in criminal statistics, investigations of female crime require more emphasis on the study of unpunished and unnoticed offenses than the criminality of men.

However, with this basic consideration our statistical problems in studying the criminality of women are by no means exhausted.

The index question regarding the movement of female criminality will have to be considered in the light of the specific nature of female crime. Our statistical considerations have already led us to a reëvaluation of the detectability and prosecution of two major offense types when committed by women. We have seen that homicide by women may not be of so public a nature as one generally assumes, and that larceny by women does not induce such coöperation on the part of the victim as it does in the cases of male offenders. Since the majority of the other offenses usually applied in the construction of crime indexes (manslaughter, aggravated assault, robbery, burglary, and auto thefts) are specifically male crimes, at least as far as overt perpetration is concerned, the outlook for a reliable index of female criminality is discouraging indeed. Only the coincidence of trends in many samples will justify conclusions on the basis of Quetelet's law of permanent relationships between discovered and undiscovered crime.

For this reason the apprehension of various authors regarding the comparability of figures from different countries[18] is not shared by the writer. Accepting the difficulties which result from differences in positive criminal law, the changing enforcement policies in various countries, and the differences in the set-up and collection of criminal statistics, the writer is of the opinion that basic agreement among the various sets of data from the largest possible number of sources—inadequate as any one may be by itself—furnishes more insight into the working of a possible common factor than any investigation of only one set of data. Discernment of a common characteristic in such various sets of data would actually be the more convincing the more the possible differences are realized.

To sum up, it will have to be kept in mind that (1) incidence figures regarding female criminality as apparent in criminal statistics will have to be supplemented wherever possible by probing into the unrecorded criminality of women, (2) the sex differential in criminal statistics permits no conclusion regarding the relation between the sizes of the real criminality of the two sexes, (3) utmost care will have to be applied in the construction of an index of female criminality because of the low degree of detectability of offenses committed by women, and (4) international comparisons are an important tool in the analysis of the sex specificity of female crime.

NOTES

1 Sellin, *Research Memorandum on Crime in the Depression*, pp. 68-69; Sellin, "The Basis of a Crime Index," *Journal of the American Institute of Criminal Law and Criminology*, XXII (1931-32), 339; Gustav Aschaffenburg, *Crime and Its Repression*, p. 158; Raymond de Ryckère, "La Criminalité Ancillaire," *Archives D'Anthropologie Criminelle*, XXI (1906), 531.

2 Lombroso, *op. cit.*, p. 187; Paul Pollitz, *Die Psychologie des Verbrechers*, p. 26.

3 Winifred Richmond, *The Adolescent Girl*, p. 124; Leale, *op. cit.*, p. 419.

4 Scheinfeld, *op. cit.*, p. 250.

5 New York City, Mayor's Committee for the Study of Sex Offenses, *Report*, p. 75.

6 William Healy, *The Individual Delinquent*, p. 144; L. Clovis Hirning, "Indecent Exposure and Other Sex Offenses," *Journal of Clinical Psychopathology*, VII (1945-46), 105.

7 New York City, Mayor's Committee for the Study of Sex Offenses, *op. cit.*, p. 74.

8 Statement is based on legal principles set forth in *Handbook of Criminal Law* by Justin Miller, p. 300.

9 Colajanni, *op. cit.*, p. 83; Bonger, *Criminality and Economic Conditions*, p. 472.

10 Kellor, *Experimental Sociology*, p. 159; Sullenger, *op. cit.*, p. 706; Barnes and Teeters, *op. cit.*, p. 569; J. Edgar Hoover, "The Women in Crime," *This Week*, the magazine section of the *Detroit News*, Oct. 17, 1937; Hans von Hentig, *Crime: Causes and Conditions*, p. 109.

11 Tarnowsky, *op. cit.*, p. 96; Parmelee, *op. cit.*, p. 245; Darrow, *op. cit.*, p. 71.

12 C. J. S. Thompson, *Poison and Poisoners*, p. 115; Arthur Griffiths, "Female Criminals," *The North American Review*, CLXI (1895), 147; Van de Warker, *op. cit.*, p. 344; A. Lacassagne, *Peine de mort et criminalité*, p. 50; Robert Heindl, "Das Weib als Mörderin," *Archiv für Kriminologie*, XCV (1934), 62; and many others.

13 Wood and Waite, *op. cit.*, p. 291.

14 Scheinfeld, *op. cit.*, p. 247.

15 Kellor, *Experimental Sociology*, p. 159; Sullenger, *op. cit.*, p. 706; Barnes and Teeters, *op. cit.*, p. 571; Scheinfeld, *op. cit.*, p. 248; C. Granier, *La Femme Criminelle*, p. 6; Bonger, *Criminality and Economic Conditions*, p. 472; Pike, *op. cit.*, p. 470; Melegari, *op. cit.*, p. 525.

16 State of New York, *Eleventh Annual Report of the Commissioner of Correction on Crime Statistics*, pp. 414, 420.

17 City Council Committee on Crime of the City of Chicago, *Report*, p. 48.

18 Ernst Roesner, "Die internationale Kriminalstatistik in ihrer methodischen Entwicklung," *Allgemeines Statistisches Archiv*, XXII (1932), 27; E. Hacker, "Internationale Kriminalstatistik," *Monatsschrift für Kriminalpsychologie und Strafrechtsreform*, XXII (1931), 269.

CHAPTER II

METHODS OF CRIME COMMISSION

In the preceding chapter an attempt was made to show that the criminality of women is largely masked and that for this reason its real extent is probably far more considerable than criminal statistics suggest. Before probing further into this question, it seems necessary to assemble detailed information regarding the ways in which women commit their crimes because the knowledge so gained will provide a new perspective for the quantitative aspect of female crime and will prove suggestive of further research in this respect.

The existing characterizations of the ways in which women commit their crimes center around the observation that women offenders are more deceitful than men. Occasionally, other characteristics are mentioned, such as lack of physical strength, cruelty, and certain specific types of victims, but compared with the general emphasis on woman's preference for indirection in the attainment of her criminal goals, they are almost negligible.

Man's complaint about woman's deceitfulness is old. Apparently the first criminological source to mention this characteristic is the famous *Malleus Maleficarum* which appeared in 1487 and in the course of time attained the status of a legal code in German witch trials. The explanation given in this medieval work is worth relating because it illustrates man's persistent effort to explain this puzzling phenomenon. Rooted in the theological preoccupations of their time, its authors pointed out that Eve was created from a curved rib of Adam's and that this origin had led to woman's predilection for lies, concealment, and ruses.[1] It would be an endless task to trace the complaint about woman's deceitfulness through the literature of the centuries, but there is no doubt that it still captures the interest of scholars and laymen, and that an impressive array of criminologists, including Healy, Arthur Griffiths, H. Ashton-Wolfe, Lombroso, Ferrero, Melegari, Aschaffenburg, Buschan, M. H. Goering, and Gross,[2] consider deceitfulness as the outstanding characteristic of female offenders.

The preponderance of male authors among the criminologists who characterize the woman offender as more deceitful than the male criminal could arouse the objection that this opinion is the expression of a male bias. It is important, therefore, to investigate whether female authors also agree on this characteristic of women criminals. Such agreement can actually be found. The oldest corresponding observation of a female penologist seems to be Susanna Meredith's, reported at the annual congress of the National Prison Association in 1889.[3] Mrs. Meredith found it to be a peculiarity of female ex-convicts who came under her care always to endeavor to suppress some facts, to deny others, and on principle to try to deceive the staff of the agency to which they applied for help. Around 1900 Dora Melegari characterized female criminality as being based on deceit.[4] In the early twenties Edith N. Burleigh and Frances R. Harris in their study of delinquent girls on parole in Massachusetts found that untruthfulness was almost universal among these girls.[5] And still later Mrs. Cecil Chesterton found occasion to say in her *Women of the Underworld* that women as a sex were fundamentally less honest and more devious than men.[6]

The characterization of greater deceitfulness is, however, by no means confined to criminal women. It has been mentioned repeatedly for women in general,[7] and it may be interesting to note that a woman of the distinction and accomplishment of Margaret Sanger once stated quite generally that concealment was one of the most legitimate of woman's arts.[8]

This agreement of male and female authors on the greater proneness of woman to deceit throws an interesting light on the validity of the belief in her greater conformity with norms and her lower participation in crime and requires, therefore, a more searching analysis.

Many explanations have been offered for this female characteristic. First of all, the lesser physical strength of woman's body

has been considered one of the reasons which make women resort
to indirection in their aggressive behavior more often than men.
In the opinion of the writer, this factor should not be overstated
at our stage of technological development. At present, physical
strength is very rarely a requirement for any task. Even the
rugged labor in foundries was sometimes arranged so that it was
possible for women to take over these jobs during the last war.
It is true, however, that in the past this may have been a factor
and its consequences in shaping behavior may still be persistent
because dissimulation and deceit have always been the methods
by which the weak and the oppressed have tried to compensate
for their lack of overt aggressive vigor.[9]

But whether or not woman's body still does force her to concealment, it should be noted that it does actually make it much
easier for her to practice deceit than does the body of man. Not
enough attention has been paid to the physiological fact that man
must achieve an erection in order to perform the sex act and will
not be able to hide his failure. His lack of positive emotion in the
sexual sphere must become overt to the partner and pretense of
sexual response is impossible for him, if it is lacking. Woman's
body, however, permits such pretense to a certain degree and lack
of orgasm does not prevent her ability to participate in the sex
act. It cannot be denied that this basic physiological difference
may well have a great influence on the degree of confidence which
the two sexes have in the possible success of concealment and thus
on their character pattern in this respect.[10]

In addition to the aftereffects of former physical necessity and
the physiological possibility in at least one important sphere of
life, there exists a normative differential between the veracity
socially expected from men and women. Our sex mores force
women to conceal every four weeks the period of menstruation.
The traditional requirements of motherhood still require many
women to misrepresent or to conceal from children sex information, at least for a certain period of time. They thus make concealment and misrepresentation in the eyes of women socially
required and commendable acts, and must condition them to a
different attitude toward veracity than men.[11]

But not only in the sexual sphere is concealment and deceit

required of women. It is also a general command of the Victorian part of our general mores. In the development of every girl, there comes a time when her natural aggressions are inhibited and forced into concealed channels. She must not fight with boys any more, she must not show them her interest in them, she must not take the active part in establishing an emotional relationship. Until recently, her chances of creating an independent existence for herself were severely limited and her economic future depended largely on getting a husband who would be able to support her, but she was not supposed to pursue one freely.[12] Thus winning out in the struggle of emotions and also in the struggle for existence implied for women deceit, not as a deviation, but as a socially prescribed form of behavior.

This interplay between physical and cultural factors seems, therefore, actually to result in a greater lack of sincerity in women than in men. For the latter it is always a deviation, for the former often a technical necessity and a social command. It is not surprising that this characteristic of the female sex should find its expression also in crime. Almost all criminals want to remain undetected, but it seems that women offenders are much better equipped for achieving this goal than are men. Most of the prevailing beliefs in woman's lower criminality will have to be reëvaluated in the light of this conclusion.

Closely connected with the observation of the greater deceitfulness of women is another one which seems to present an interesting dilemma. A few authors mention that women criminals have strange fits of veracity which lead to the detection of their crimes. It has been said that often women offenders are under a compulsion to talk about their secrets to at least one person, are lead to treachery under the impact of jealousy or personal antagonism, and "turn state evidence" in order to save their own skins.[13]

These observations seem to contradict the general characteristic of female insincerity, but on further consideration this is not the case. First of all, only a small number of authors have produced observations to this effect, and in all social behavior exceptions to the norm can be noted. Since the observation of deceitfulness is almost universal, the observation of veracity, however, confined to a few authors, it seems to the writer that they may well refer to exceptional cases which have been unduly generalized. Furthermore, most of these cases of so-called veracity are cases of treachery committed by women informers acting from spite or fear, and treachery is in itself an act of insincerity and deceit.

Another piece of apparent counterevidence resolves itself similarly on closer consideration. If one is to believe certain authors, women are not careful in covering their tracks. Hans Gross advises investigators to bear in mind that women are loath to destroy evidence for emotional reasons. Incriminating letters and actual corpora delicti are said to be more often found in the cases of female offenders than in the cases of male criminals. It has also been said that the dress, long nails, and perfume of women often lead to the detection of female offenders. No women can supposedly bring themselves to wear rough boots in order to avoid leaving the specific feminine traces of their footprints. Their fashionably long nails make scratches when searching for valuables. Use of powder and make-up leaves many traces which lead police experts to the right track.[14] It may be questioned, however, whether this is really a general characteristic. Of course, since women wear a type of shoes very different from those worn by men, since they use powder and make-up while men do not, and since they often, but by no means always, have long fingernails while men have them closely clipped, it must occur that those who are caught are often tracked down on the basis of these characteristics while men are not. But whether such tracks are left by the majority of female offenders or only by those who blunder, we have no way of telling. The foregoing observations may well be based on a biased sample unrepresentative of the bulk of female offenders.

A few male authors have further mentioned greater cruelty as a characteristic of female crime,[15] but the supporting evidence is so scanty and uncorroborated by other observations that these references seem to reflect more the surprise of the authors about the seeming contradiction between the female stereotype of behavior and the individual deviation than the discovery of a characteristic of female crime.

An apparently more substantiated observation regarding the

modus operandi of female offenders is related to the types of victims which they seem to choose. Children, husbands, family members in general, and lovers have been mentioned in this respect.[16] In this connection it must not be overlooked that most legal systems contain one crime, infanticide, which by its definition in the law can only be committed by "mothers" on their children. Since there exists no corresponding crime for men, the material on which these observations are based is somewhat loaded. Consideration of woman's roles in our society, however, suggests that the observations may be valid. Woman's sphere was, and in many instances still is, the home. The victims of her offenses against the person must be largely drawn from those with whom she has contacts on that basis. Furthermore, our social customs which prevent woman from taking the initiative in establishing contacts with persons whom she does not know may well work also against her attacking strangers in the manner of men. It seems plausible, therefore, that children, husbands, lovers, and members of the family circle should figure more frequently among the victims of woman criminals than among those of male offenders. This seemingly logical conclusion, however, should not be overemphasized. It has even been said that women steal mostly from persons whom they know,[17] but the rather extensive number of female pickpockets and the even more extensive number of female shoplifters suggest that female thieves do by no means labor under any such handicap.[18]

In addition to the limitations of her contacts, it is also the nature of woman's social roles as such which leads her to prefer certain types of victims. In our culture the care of children is woman's task. This function permits women to select children as the victims of their crimes in ways in which men could never indulge without arousing suspicion. This is a possible aspect of female sex offenses which has remained practically unnoticed. It has been recognized, however, in the cases of slow killings of children by women called baby farmers,[19] and it has even been noticed that women have attracted children into alleyways and taken earrings or other little pieces of jewelry from them.[20] There are thus some indications that women prefer children and persons with whom they are related or in otherwise close contact as the victims of their crimes, which in many instances must decrease the coöperation of the victim with the law-enforcing authorities.

In summary, it can be said that observations reported in the literature and biological as well as cultural analyses suggest two general characteristics of female crime: (1) great deceitfulness of the offenders and (2) preference for certain groups of victims such as children in general and members of the family circle or persons with whom they have other personal ties. Both characteristics must influence adversely the detectability of female offenses and thereby the value of criminal statistics.

In the following pages the attempt will be made to put these tentative conclusions to the test of an analysis of the behavior of female offenders in the various types of crime. To this purpose the available material in the literature has been assembled and will be presented in integrated form.

NOTES

[1] Gregory Zilboorg, "Masculine and Feminine," *Psychiatry*, VII (1944), 262-63.
[2] William Healy and Mary Tenney Healy, *Pathological Lying, Accusation, and Swindling*, p. 261; Griffiths, *op. cit.*, p. 143; H. Ashton-Wolfe, *The Forgotten Clue*, p. 250; Lombroso and Ferrero, *op. cit.*, pp. 141-48; Melegari, *op. cit.*, p. 532; Aschaffenburg, *op. cit.*, p. 158; Buschan, *op. cit.*, p. 52; M. H. Göring, "Kriminalpsychologie," in *Handbuch der Vergleichenden Psychologie*, III, Abteilung 2, p. 162; Gross, *op. cit.*, p. 400. In regard to deceitfulness in female witnesses, see Francis L. Wellman, *The Art of Cross-Examination*, p. 123.
[3] Susanna Meredith, "Some Peculiarities of Criminals," *Proceedings of the Annual Congress of the National Prison Association of the United States, Held at Nashville, Nov. 16-20, 1889*, pp. 222-23.
[4] Melegari, *op. cit.*, p. 532.
[5] Edith N. Burleigh and Frances R. Harris, *The Delinquent Girl*, p. 13.
[6] Mrs. Cecil Chesterton, *Women of the Underworld*, p. 11.
[7] Earl Barnes, *Woman in Modern Society*, p. 22; Helen Jerome, *The Secret of Woman*, p. 69; M. Esther Harding, *The Way of all Women*, pp. 11, 13, 32, 33.
[8] Margaret Sanger, *Happiness in Marriage*, p. 59.
[9] Finot, *op. cit.*, p. 286; Lombroso and Ferrero, *op. cit.*, p. 144; Guglielmo Ferrero, "Le Mensonge et la Véracité chez la Femme," *Archives D'Anthropologie Criminelle*, VIII (1893), 138.
[10] Clara Thompson, "Cultural Pressures in the Psychology of Women," *Psychiatry*, V (1942), 333.
[11] Lombroso and Ferrero, *op. cit.*, pp. 144-45; Gross, *op. cit.*, p. 400; Ferrero, *op. cit.*, p. 138.

12 Jerome, *op. cit.*, p. 69; Thompson, *op. cit.*, p. 335; Lombroso and Ferrero, *op. cit.*, p. 146.

13 Ferrero, *op. cit.*, pp. 145-46; Netley Lucas, *Crook Janes—A Study of the Woman Criminal the World Over*, p. 8; Cecil Bishop, *From Information Received*, pp. 40-41.

14 Gross, *op. cit.*, p. 440; Ashton-Wolfe, *op. cit.*, p. 251.

15 Paul Aubry, "De L'Homicide Commis par la Femme," *Archives D'Anthropologie Criminelle*, VI (1891), 284; Erich Wulffen, *Das Weib als Sexualverbrecherin*, pp. 256 ff; Lombroso and Ferrero, *op. cit.*, p. 102.

16 *Compte General de l'Administration de la Justice Criminelle pendant l'Année 1880*, "Rapport au Président de la République sur l'Administration Criminelle en France de 1826 à 1880," p. lxvii; Granier, *op. cit.*, p. 243; Charles Mercier, *Crime and Criminals*, p. 189; Melegari, *op. cit.*, p. 530.

17 Granier, *op. cit.*, p. 242.

18 Phil. Farley, *Criminals of America*, pp. 53-65, 206-10; Bishop, *From Information Received*, pp. 163-67; A. Antheaume, *Le Roman d'une Épidémie Parisienne La Kleptomanie?* pp. 23-24, 140-53.

19 Melegari, *op. cit.*, pp. 528-29.

20 Granier, *op. cit.*, p. 243.

CHAPTER III

CRIMES AGAINST THE PERSON

In this chapter the available information on the ways in which women commit murder, infanticide, criminal assaults, false accusation, and sex offenses against children will be presented in order to examine the detectability of these crimes in such cases.

Homicide.

There seems to be almost unanimous agreement among criminologists that the woman who kills uses poison more often than any other means. Observations to this effect have come from many countries and cover a large span of time.[1] Since these observations are mostly reported without corroborating figures, the writer has analyzed the first hundred cases presented in Pauline Tarnowsky's monograph on female murderers as to the method of killing employed. Among these hundred cases of female homicide, poison was used 35 times while no other method was used more than 16 times.[2] The Tarnowsky material suggests, therefore, the correctness of the impression that women use poison more frequently than any other means of committing homicide. But not only do they use it more than any other means, they also use it more frequently than men. In an investigation of all poison cases which came to the attention of the French courts from 1825 to 1880, Lacassagne found that the participation of women had considerably increased over the time span covered. In the period 1875-80, 6.8 out of every 10 killers were women, and a similar preponderance of women among apprehended poisoners, namely, 6.3 out of every 10, has been reported for the United States.[3] It seems, therefore, that the cumulative evidence of modern scientists does little but reaffirm Reginald Scot's statement of 1584, that women were "the greatest practicers of poisoning and more . . . given thereunto than men."[4]

The poisons which women employ in their homicidal attacks on human life are rather few in number. Outstanding and most frequently used of them all are derivations of arsenic. Next to it, but by far less often used, are cyanide, bichloride of mercury, and corrosive sublimate.[5] Within the last years thallium has been reported as increasingly used by German poisoners.[6] The reasons for the frequency with which arsenic is used are the following: It is easily obtainable as an insecticide or rat poison for apparently legitimate uses in the household. It is easily disguised in food or drink, and the signs and symptoms which it produces are often deceptively similar to those caused by all diseases which lead to gastroenteritis, such as cholera, typhoid, intestinal flu, and others. The detectability of this poison is particularly low when the victim has already been suffering from a chronic disease which suggests a natural cause of death. Perhaps more important than all these, it has the endorsement of history, which makes it the obvious poison for the lay person.[7]

If we consider these qualities of arsenic in connection with woman's social roles as the preparer of meals and the nurse of the sick, it appears obvious why it should have become the favorite weapon of female murderers. The woman who buys a gun is suspect, a woman who buys an insecticide such as, for instance, flypaper is not; a woman who resorts to overt attack will meet with physical defense, a woman who serves a meal will not; and a woman who nurses her victim in sickness will enjoy the confidence of the doctor rather than arouse his suspicion. Thus, procurement as well as use of this favorite weapon in female homicide is easily concealed and permits more than any other criminal weapon the deception of the victim and those interested in him. To be sure, men who have similar opportunities to administer poisons in their homicidal attacks, such as physicians and druggists, resort equally to them.[8] The fact remains, however, that physicians and druggists represent only a very small fraction of the male population, while to be a homemaker is the social role of the vast majority of the women in our society. We must conclude, therefore, that so far, at least in the field of homicide, the general contention that woman's crimes are more frequently and more successfully masked than the crimes of man seems to be corroborated.

This seems to apply, however, only to women acting alone.[9] When women act in complicity with others, poison seems to be less frequently resorted to, and the method of procedure often assumes a more overt character, increasing the detectability of the offense. This difference in the modus operandi between homicides committed by women alone and homicides in which women participate only as accomplices becomes clear in those cases in which the social role of the woman and the character of the victim would suggest the use of poison with all its advantages from the criminal point of view, but where she works in cooperation with a man. Case material reported by European authors throws an interesting light on this phenomenon. They suggest that when a woman enlists the help of a lover or a son in the attack on her husband's life, other means than poison are employed and it is resorted to only if the woman instigator despairs of getting help from her male accomplice and tries to finish the crime herself.[10]

This investigation of the modus operandi in cases of complicity suggests, therefore, a revision of the opinion expressed by some authors regarding the influence of woman's role as an instigator on the validity of statistics as far as homicide is concerned. The detectability of homicides where the woman acts in complicity with men is greater than in cases where she acts alone.

Next to the means employed, the type of victim particularly exposed to female homicides deserves further attention for an evaluation of criminal statistics. It has been mentioned in Chapter II that there are some indications that children and persons to whom women offenders are related or with whom they are in otherwise close contact loom largely among their victims. With regard to homicide, the prevalence of poison among the means employed indicates clearly that the group of victims who can be easily reached by this criminal weapon of the woman murderer must in most instances belong to the household. The general observation reported above seems, therefore, corroborated for this offense.

How seldom attacks on the lives of persons belonging to their household are traced to the female murderers is suggested by those cases in which women who were finally caught and brought to trial were discovered to have poisoned other family members as well as the victim whose death had aroused suspicion. To mention only two cases from more recent years, investigation of the death of her son revealed in 1931 that a woman in this country had poisoned her husband, a nephew, and a boarder before she poisoned her own child, and in Austria the wife of an engineer was convicted in 1938 of having killed in the years 1932 to 1936 in this order her husband, one of her children, an aunt, and a friend, with thallium, with only the fourth poisoning arousing suspicion.[11] These cases, which could be easily duplicated from periods further back, show how great the chances of escape must be in those instances in which women murderers confine themselves to only one homicide in the family circle.

In general, it can be concluded that homicide committed by women can be called secret murder and that the general observations about the highly masked character of female crime are well substantiated by the modus operandi of the woman who kills.

Baby Farming.

This type of offense is actually a form of homicide in which only young children are the victims and in which the means resorted to are not poisons or any other weapon, but simply criminal neglect and starvation. It has, however, been customarily regarded as a special phenomenon, which is the reason for its special treatment in this investigation. An offense which has lost its importance in the last decades, it played a great role in the nineteenth and the beginning of the twentieth century and aroused much indignation and legislative reaction when it was brought to public attention.[12]

Baby farmers were women to whom unmarried mothers turned over their infants, ostensibly to have the children cared for and brought up against the payment of a lump sum. Actually there was a quiet understanding that the children should be made to die inconspicuously. Neglect and insufficient food soon weakened the children so that they succumbed easily to diseases, and the overburdened practitioners in rural districts, where these baby farms were usually located, seldom had time enough to probe carefully into the death causes of the children. This malpractice is said to have existed in all countries,[13] and scandalous revelations in Paris and London indicated that it had attained the proportions of a veritable industry. As late as 1916, it was discovered that it was still going strong in Chicago.[14]

A detailed discussion of this crime does not seem to be necessary any more because of its now almost obsolete character. However, the type of victim and the methods employed again show the use (or more correctly, the abuse) of a typically female function, child care, as a cover for the criminal offense. They also show the highly masked character of the procedure, and the noncoöperation of the victim or those who should have been interested in him with the law-enforcing authorities. That this crime was, therefore, by no means adequately reflected in criminal statistics is obvious, which is another instance of the highly masked nature of the criminality of women.

Infanticide.

This specifically female crime is declining in incidence because of the increasing practice of birth control in ever wider strata of the population, and will probably continue to do so in the future. It is, however, not yet obsolete and therefore requires more attention from the criminologist than baby farming.

The various methods which characterize this offense have been described so often and with such similarity that it makes little difference whether one consults references going back as far as 1820 and 1836 or as recent as 1934 and 1939. American, English, French, and German authors all stress suffocation, strangulation, and the infliction of wounds or fractures to the skull as the most frequent forms of infanticide. Poisoning, burning, drowning, and willful omissions of the necessary care, such as exposure to cold temperature, withholding of food, or neglect of the consequences of accident, are also, but not unanimously, mentioned as modi operandi for this offense.[15] It must not be overlooked that some of these modi operandi can also be ways and means of disposing of the body. Drowning in kitchen water and in toilets, inflicting of wounds while forcing the infant's body through the outlet of a toilet or the opening of an outhouse, and particularly burning are probably more often attempts of the mother to cover her tracks than methods of killing.[16]

These observations are largely based on the individual experiences of physicians, as planfully collected statistical material is scarce. The one clearly statistical investigation which has come to the attention of the writer, however, corroborates the impression of all authors that suffocation and strangulation occur more often than any of the other methods reported. They were found to have occurred in 25 cases out of a sample of 49.[17]

Suffocation is brought about in various ways. The nose and the mouth of the infant may be covered with the mother's hand, a handkerchief, or a pillow; cloth or feathers may be stuffed into the throat of the child; his face may be pressed into a pillow, or it may be covered completely with a blanket.[18]

Strangulation is effected by constricting the neck of the infant by ligature or manual compression. A piece of string, a ribbon, or even the umbilical cord may be used.[19]

Drowning is usually done in a toilet pan, bathtub, laundry sink, or kitchen pail.[20]

Infliction of wounds is generally done with instruments which are normally in the hands of women, such as needles, scissors, and kitchen knives. The mothers who use them are often cooks or garment workers. It has been observed that the woman who kills her newborn infant in such ways usually does not finish the job in one thrust, slash, or stab, but repeats the attack, often hitting the same spot over and over again. This repetition of the attack has been said to give the impression that the mother had not been master of herself and had acted in blind fury.[21]

The common characteristic of almost all the methods reported is the possibility of executing them without any type of special preparation. The social situation of the mothers who resort to infanticide makes this easily understandable. They are usually unmarried girls without means who are dominated by the idea of concealing their pregnancy. A large contingent of these offenders is composed of live-in maids who are afraid of losing their jobs. Their main interest lies in the concealment of their physical changes. Morning sickness and dizzy spells have to be suppressed or explained away. Employers and neighbors have to be watched to see if they have noticed anything. Thus, all their energies are consumed by their efforts to keep their situation secret.[22] When the moment of delivery arrives, they are unprepared and, continuing their mental trend of concealment, they resort to those two places where they can have privacy, their room or a toilet where they submit to their labor under the obsession to remain undiscovered. They have to suppress their own pains, they are without assistance, and when the child appears they are maddened by the fear that its cry may be heard. So their first reaction toward the child is to prevent its crying.[23] They try to smother it in the bed, they put their hands over its mouth, or try by immediate killing to prevent its being heard. Hence, the prevalence of suffocation and strangulation and perhaps also the fury with which they attack the child when they resort to instruments.

The spots in which the bodies of the infants are usually concealed are very simple and obvious. The sewer pipe, the cesspool of an outhouse, a box in the mother's room, and even garbage and ash cans are used.[24]

These various aspects of the modus operandi in infanticides pose a puzzling question for the student of criminal statistics. The predominant characteristic of the female offender, the inclination to concealment, is perhaps nowhere more clearly expressed than in this crime. The social situation of the mother, however, and her physical state of exhaustion after an unassisted delivery make it impossible for her to adequately cover her tracks. The body of the victim, though small and no obstacle to easy concealment, is hardly ever successfully disposed of. Furthermore, it is not easy to conceal the state of pregnancy itself.[25] It may have been comparatively easy in the days of the hoop skirt and a different beauty ideal for the female figure, but in our time the prevailing emphasis on slenderness and the modern fashions in clothing make pregnancy certainly a noticeable condition. Therefore it seems that, at least at the present time, infanticide should be a rather highly detectable offense. The spread of birth control, however, robs it of its index value because it influences the movement of the infanticide rate independently of the development of other rates of female crime. Its relation between apparent and real criminality may be close, but its index value is questionable.

Aggravated Assault.

Regarding this offense, general observations as well as case material about women offenders is scarce. Only one method of committing this offense has been reported as specifically feminine, the throwing of sulphuric acid in order to disfigure the victim.[26] According to most authors who have studied this offense, the victim is usually an unfaithful lover; Puibaraud, however, has expressed the opinion that it is more frequently the successful rival than the lover who is the victim of the attack.[27]

In both cases the aim is interference with a competing emotional relationship by means of destroying the physical attractiveness of one of its partners, and the act is based on a desire for revenge. A few cases, one of which has been reported twice in the literature, however, suggest the possibility of another motive. Apparently, it can also be potential rather than actual unfaithfulness of the lover which prompts the offender into action. In such instances the disfiguration has the purpose of making the lover undesirable for any potential rival and thus securing him permanently for the offender.[28]

In the usual type of case, the disruption of the original ties between the offender and the lover or the antagonism between her and her rival makes it impossible for the woman offender to approach the victim in the privacy of a home, as is characteristic of the female murderer. She has, therefore, to resort to a more public place for the crime, and a street, a public park, or a restaurant seems to be the most frequent scene of this offense.[29] Only the time of the offense appears to contain an element of deceit: it seems to take place mostly after dark.

Thus, the criminal aim as well as the social situation contributes to making this crime a highly detectable offense. It must, by the very intention of the offender, leave obvious traces and lead to grave injury. It is usually based on mutual antagonism between the offender and the victim or at least a person vitally interested in him, so that coöperation from the side of the victim with the law-enforcing authorities is assured. Its real extent is, therefore, in all probability adequately reflected in criminal statistics, and it has all the characteristics required for index quality.

All these considerations hold true, however, only for those cases in which the method used is the throwing of sulphuric acid. Regarding other types of aggravated assault committed by women, no specific observations seem to have been reported in the literature. Thus, the question whether the general attitude of male protectiveness and chivalry does not work against the coöperation of the victim with the agents of the law in these other instances cannot be answered with the material available. Since vitriol throwing is not reported separately but together with all other types of aggravated assault, we again have an offense which, under the present practice of recording, leaves us at a loss to know whether its real extent is adequately reflected in criminal statistics and whether we can assign it index quality if it is committed by women.

False Accusation.

This is a crime of considerable interest for our investigation because the greater deceitfulness of women, if really existent, should certainly find its expression in an offense which by definition consists of misrepresentation and falsification. Actually, no lesser authority than William Healy has stated that women are more prone to commit this offense than are men.[30] Furthermore, there is agreement among the authors who have paid any attention at all to this crime that its content shows a specific pattern if it is committed by women. No matter whether the motive of the offense is revenge, concealment of actual misconduct, or a pathological flight from reality, the content of the false accusations committed by women is apparently, in the vast majority of cases, an alleged sexual attack on the accuser.[31] Even when the content of the accusation is of a different nature, the motive is said to have almost always a sexual tinge.[32] The statements containing the false accusation are often made without much original planning or elaboration but, after having aroused attention, they are developed in great detail and often maintained at the police station and in court. They may lead to official investigations and to arrests of innocent persons, but may end up in the conviction of the accuser for perjury or in her being adjudged delinquent.[33]

The offenders are said to be usually young girls still in the state of pubescence,[34] or women suffering from hysteria.[35]

In the United States, some of these crimes take place in an atmosphere of race antagonism. White women may accuse negro men of sexual attacks in order to free themselves from the consequences of illicit sex conduct; they may do so in order to get rid of a negro lover of whom they are tired, or in order to avoid social ostracism after discovery; neurotics may interpret an innocent action by a negro as a sexual attack.[36] The possibility of such false accusations has been suggested by various cases of white women charging rape against colored men which resulted in acquittals.

From the angle of criminal statistics, the following factors must be considered in an evaluation of the detectability of this offense. In our culture with its sex taboos, the allegation of a sex attack establishes immediate sympathy with the accuser and prejudice against her victim. Our general protectiveness toward women also comes forcefully into play. If the accusation is made by a white woman against a negro, race antagonism is added, and sympathy with the offender as well as prejudice against her victim will be intensified. The chances of the victim's putting forth an effective defense are thus greatly impaired. The two possible means of such a defense, proof of the virginity of the accuser or an alibi, are severely limited because the first is not available in those cases in which the accuser is not virginal and the second is very difficult to prove in an unimpeachable fashion. It is, therefore, not surprising that among the cases in the Healy material virgins seem to figure comparatively largely among the offenders, since this group alone offers a definite opportunity for convincing proof of the falsity of their accusations of a completed sex attack.[37] A fair chance of detection seems also to exist in the cases of neurotics. Such persons may repeat the offense so often that they arouse suspicion and are finally caught.[38]

It seems, therefore, that only the false accusations of virginal girls and of neurotics justify a reasonable expectation of discovery, and that we have no way of telling how many other false accusations are committed by women. Thus, adequate reflection of its real extent in criminal statistics as well as index quality of this offense must be as much if not more seriously questioned as for the other crimes of women against the person.

Sex Offenses against Children.

Another type of criminal attack against the person committed by women is violations of the sexual integrity of children. Considering its potential harmfulness, this offense type is disturbingly neglected by criminological research. Here again the cover of one of woman's social roles, her modus operandi, and the type of victim seem to mask female criminality to a very high degree. It has only to be considered that the sex violation of a little girl by a male offender will leave the definite physical trace of the rupture of the hymen while the sexual attack of a woman against a boy will leave no trace whatsoever unless a social disease has been imparted.[39] Furthermore, handling the body of a child by a woman will in most instances be accepted as a function of child care or as an expression of normal affection. Coming from a man, it will often arouse suspicion as a sexual act. It is, therefore, understandable that medical and criminological literature contains only a very few references to this offense. The writer was unable to locate more than one paper dealing specifically with this phenomenon, and significantly enough that paper reports only on cases in which the sex attack of the woman offender had resulted in the venereal infection of the child.[40] In how many cases attacks of this kind do not lead to such a discovery-promoting consequence must remain open to conjecture. However, it is probable that only a very small fraction of these offenses ever reach the attention of the law.

Sex acts may also be covered by sham measures of children's discipline. Since the discipline of small children is largely in the hands of the mother or a mother's substitute such as a maid, a governess, a nursery school or kindergarten teacher, we are here faced with still another field of possible female crime which, because of the cover of a social role and the obvious inability of the victim to enlist the protection of the law, must remain practically undetected.[41]

NOTES

1 Griffiths, *op. cit.*, p. 147; Van de Warker, *op. cit.*, p. 344; C. J. S. Thompson, *op. cit.*, p. 115; Edmond Locard, *Le Crime et les Criminels*, p. 234; A. Lacassagne, "Notes Statistiques sur L'Empoisonnement Criminel en France," *Archives D'Anthropologie Criminelle*, I (1886), 262; Hargrave L. Adam, *Woman and Crime*, p. 44; John C. Goodwin, *Sidelights on Criminal Matters*, p. 26; Mercier, *op. cit.*, p. 189; Wilhelm Sauer, *Kriminalsoziologie*, II, p. 227; Gross, *op. cit.*, p. 463; Hübner, "Kriminalpsychologisches über das weibliche Geschlecht," *Allgemeine Zeitschrift für Psychiatrie*, LXIX (1912), 278; Heindl, *op. cit.*, p. 62.

2 Tarnowsky, *op. cit.*, pp. 104-333.

3 Lacassagne, "Notes Statistiques sur L'Empoisonnement Criminel en France," pp. 263-64; C. J. S. Thompson, *op. cit.*, p. 116.

4 Reginald Scot, *The discouerie of witchcraft*, p. 116.

5 William D. McNally, *Medical Jurisprudence and Toxicology*, p. 168; William F. Boos, *The Poison Trail*, p. 278.

6 Hans Steidle, "Thallium, das neue Mord und Selbstmordgift," *Medizinische Welt*, XIII (1939), 1557; K. Böhmer, "Kriminelle Thalliumvergiftung," *Deutsche Zeitschrift für die Gesamte Gerichtliche Medizin*, XXX (1938), 146-47.

7 Alfred S. Taylor, *Medical Jurisprudence*, p. 82; McNally, *op. cit.*, p. 168; Albert W. Bryan, "Arsenic Poisoning," *The Wisconsin Medical Journal*, XXXVIII (1939), 545; Boos, *op. cit.*, p. 279.

8 C. Ainsworth Mitchell, *Science and the Criminal*, pp. 190-96; Edmund Pearson, *Murder at Smutty Nose and other Murders*, pp. 135-47; George Dilnot, *The Story of Scotland Yard*, pp. 319-25; Liselotte Herx, *Der Giftmord, insbesondere der Giftmord durch Frauen*, p. 9.

9 Heindl, *op. cit.*, p. 62.

10 Scipio Sighele, *Le Crime A Deux*, pp. 61-63, 87-89, 116-20; Aubry, *op. cit.*, p. 276; Hein Schröder, "Anlage und Umwelt in ihrer Bedeutung für die Verwahrlosung weiblicher Jugendlicher," *Allgemeine Zeitschrift für die Psychiatrie und ihre Grenzgebiete*, CXII-CXIII (1939), Supplement 12, p. 225.

11 McNally, *op. cit.*, p. 168; Steidle, *op. cit.*, p. 1557.

12 C. C. Carstens, "Neglected Children," in "Child," *Encyclopaedia of the Social Sciences*, III (1930), 404.

13 R. de Ryckère, *La Femme en Prison et devant la Mort*, p. 184; Wulffen, *op. cit.*, p. 308.

14 Melegari, *op. cit.*, p. 529; Robert J. Parr, *The Baby Farmer*, p. 21 ff.; Benjamin Waugh, "Babyfarming," *The Contemporary Review*, LVII (1890), 700-14; Frances H. Low, "A Remedy for Babyfarming," *The Fortnightly Review*, LXIII, New Series (1898), 280-86; Arthur Alden Guild, *Baby Farms in Chicago*, 27 pp.

15 William Hutchinson, *A Dissertation on Infanticide in Its Relations to Physiology and Jurisprudence* (London, 1820), pp. 19, 80-82; William Cummin, *The Proofs of Infanticide* (London, 1836), pp. 83-91; Allan McLane Hamilton and Lawrence Godkin, *A System of Legal Medicine* (New York, 1894), II, pp. 491-95; J. H. Morton, "Female Homicides," *The Journal of Mental Science*, LXXX (1934), 69; P. Brouardel, *L'infanticide* (Paris, 1897), pp. 78-135; Albin Haberda, "Zur Lehre vom Kindesmorde," *Beiträge zur Gerichtlichen Medizin*, I (1911), pp. 77, 160-91; E. Ungar, "Der Nachweis des Kindesmordes" in *Gerichtsärztliche und polizeiärztliche Technik* (Wiesbaden, 1914), pp. 632-39;

G. Puppe, "Zur Psychologie und Prophylaxe des Kindesmordes," *Deutsche Medizinische Wochenschrift*, XLIII (1917), 610-11.

[16] Hamilton and Godkin, *op. cit.*, p. 493; Brouardel, *op. cit.*, p. 90.

[17] Puppe, *op. cit.*, pp. 610-11.

[18] Hamilton and Godkin, *op. cit.*, p. 491.

[19] *Ibid.*, p. 492; Brouardel, *op. cit.*, p. 87.

[20] Morton, *op. cit.*, p. 69; Brouardel, *op. cit.*, p. 90.

[21] Brouardel, *op. cit.*, pp. 115-17.

[22] James Devon, *The Criminal and the Community*, p. 155.

[23] Granier, *op. cit.*, p. 107.

[24] Healy, *op. cit.*, p. 636; Devon, *op. cit.*, p. 156; Bishop, *Women and Crime*, p. 217; Clara Thorbecke, "Über jugendliche Kindesmörderinnen," *Archiv für Kriminologie*, LXXVII (1925), 54-55.

[25] Oiva Elo, "Der Kindesmord in der Kriminalstatistik," *Deutsche Zeitschrift für die Gesamte Gerichtliche Medizin*, XXXII (1939-40), 8.

[26] Adeline M. Bedford, "Fifteen Years' Work in a Female Convict Prison," *The Nineteenth Century and After*, LXVIII (July-Dec. 1910), 619; Alexander Jassny, "Zur Psychologie der Verbrecherin," *Archiv für Kriminal-Anthropologie*, XLII (1911), 101; Emil Hey, "Die Vitriolseuche in Russland," *Archiv für Kriminal-Anthropologie*, LVII (1914), 312.

[27] Granier, *op. cit.*, p. 181; Jassny, *op. cit.*, p. 101; Hey, *op. cit.*, p. 312; Louis Puibaraud, "La Femme Criminelle," *La Grande Revue*, XII (1899), 415.

[28] Sighele, *op. cit.*, pp. 80-82; Hey, *op. cit.*, p. 314; H. B. Irving, *A Book of Remarkable Criminals*, pp. 244-69.

[29] Hey, *op. cit.*, p. 313.

[30] William Healy and Mary Tenney Healy, *op. cit.*, p. 261.

[31] Devon, *op. cit.*, pp. 148-49; William Healy and Mary Tenney Healy, *op. cit.*, pp. 35, 182, 198, 214; Erich Harnack, *Die gerichtliche Medizin*, p. 374; Karl Birnbaum, "Die sexuellen Falschbeschuldigungen der Hysterischen," *Archiv für Kriminal-Anthropologie*, LXIV (1915), 1-39; Siegfried Weinberg, "Über den Einfluss der Geschlechtsfunktionen auf die weibliche Kriminalität," *Juristisch-psychiatrische Grenzfragen*, VI, Heft 1 (1907), 14.

[32] Hans Georg Teichmann, *Meineidige und Meineidssituationen*, p. 20; and others.

[33] Bishop, *Women and Crime*, p. 19; Healy, *op. cit.*, pp. 614, 615, 740; William Healy and Mary Tenney Healy, *op. cit.*, p. 173.

[34] Cyril Lodovic Burt, *The Young Delinquent*, p. 368; Otto Lipmann, "Zur Beurteilung von Aussagen junger Mädchen," *Archiv für Kriminal-Anthropologie*, LXXIX (1926), 54.

[35] William Healy and Mary Tenney Healy, *op. cit.*, p. 35; Lombroso and Ferrero, *op. cit.*, p. 524; Birnbaum, "Die sexuellen Falschbeschuldigungen der Hysterischen," *in toto*; Johannes Bresler, "Die pathologische Anschuldigung," *Juristisch-psychiatrische Grenzfragen*, V, No. 8 (1907), 12; Mönkemöller, "Sittlichkeitsdelikt und Psychologie der Aussage," *Archiv für Kriminal-Anthropologie*, LXXVIII (1926), 130.

[36] Gunnar Myrdal, *An American Dilemma*, II, pp. 972-73; Monroe N. Work (Ed.), *Negro Year Book 1931-32*, p. 292; *Negro Year Book 1937-38*, p. 148.

[37] Healy, *op. cit.*, pp. 614-15, 714; William Healy and Mary Tenney Healy, *op. cit.*, pp. 173, 182, 198, 203.

[38] William Healy and Mary Tenney Healy, *op. cit.*, pp. 163, 214; Birnbaum, "Die sexuellen Falschbeschuldigungen der Hysterischen," pp. 29-30.

[39] Harnack, *op. cit.*, p. 54.

[40] P. A. Lop, "Attentats à la Pudeur des Femmes sur des Petits Garçons," *Archives d'Anthropologie Criminelle*, X (1895), 37-42.

[41] Reinhold Stade, *Frauentypen aus dem Gefängnisleben*, p. 229.

CHAPTER IV

CRIMES AGAINST PROPERTY

Following the procedure established in the preceding chapter with regard to crimes against the person, the investigation presented below will test the influence of the modus operandi upon the detectability of female crime against property for various specific offense types.

Robbery and Burglary.

These crimes are considered specifically male offenses since they represent the pursuit of monetary gain by overt action and thus combine in the criminal sphere two roles which in our culture have been generally assigned to men. Therefore, material on female offenders is scarce for these two types of crime. This scarcity is particularly pronounced for robbery, and the few cases reported in the literature show women either as accomplices of male offenders who use them as watchers or decoys, or as exponents of the masculinization of female crime which some criminologists have been expecting since Colajanni in 1889 predicted a development to that effect.[1]

It is interesting to note that those cases of female robbery which seem to express a tendency toward masculinization come from the Middle or Far West, where social conditions have favored the assumption of male pursuits by women, not only within, but also outside the sphere of the law. The female offenders usually retain some trace of femininity, however, and even so glaring an example of masculinization as the "Michigan Babies," an all-woman gang of robbers in Chicago, shows a typically feminine trait in the modus operandi. This was a group of holdup women who operated on the banks of Lake Michigan at night and used their most attractive member as a decoy to lure men into their traps.[2] This abuse of a characteristically female sex role for criminal purposes will come up again in practically all our analyses of the procedure of female offenders in predatory crimes. The trick seems to be used equally by women working alone and by women who work together with men. Because it capitalizes on the desire of the victim to engage in illicit sex conduct, it works strongly against his willingness to coöperate with the police. Thus, it lowers the detectability of all offenses in which it is employed.

The woman who engages in burglary is usually an accomplice working with male burglars. She confines herself to auxiliary participation, acting mostly as a spy, decoy, or watcher. Again she is assisted by the opportunities offered through sham performances of typically female roles. Posing as a maid, a woman can obtain information about the layout of the premises, the habits of her intended victims, and the location of possible loot which would be inaccessible to the male burglars with whom she is associated. As a decoy, she tries to make the acquaintance of a night watchman a few days ahead of time and arrange a tryst which will keep him from making his rounds at the hour for which the burglary is planned. Because of the immoral implication which a denouncement of this maneuver would throw on his conduct, the watchman will afterward be tempted to conceal the truth from the police and thus may withhold important information which might lead to the arrest of the criminals. Even if the burglars should be caught, however, the reticence of the watchman may help their woman accomplice to remain undetected.[3] As watchers, women have been reported to use the female appeal to male protectiveness by posing as motorists who have had an automobile breakdown for which they need the help of a mechanic. Such a woman asks approaching persons, particularly policemen, to get one from the nearest garage, thereby removing them effectively from the scene of the burglary.[4]

Instances of women committing burglaries without male collaboration are scarce, and those which have been observed seem to have arisen from abnormal situations existing only for limited periods of time. In this category belong especially those wartime cases in which the absence of their male accomplices has forced women to establish themselves independently, and therefore more overtly in this line of criminal pursuits.[5] More important in this type of crime is a group of women who are usually designated as "hotel rats." They are professionals who under the disguise of hotel guests go after their prey. They spend much time in the lobbies and dining rooms, watch the guests in order to find out which promise the richest loot, and at mealtimes or at night force their way into the hotel rooms of their victims. They usually are of distinguished appearance, occupy expensive rooms, and take care to arouse no suspicion. At night they may wear dark pajamas because such colors make them inconspicuous if they are met in the corridors. Further deception in appearance is also achieved by their wearing silk housecoats which, if they are seen to leave a room other than their own, directs speculations into misleading channels.[6]

This extensive use of her sex roles by the female offender in robbery and burglary decreases considerably her risk of being caught. If the woman offender uses her sex as a bait for the victim, he may not impart his knowledge of her identity or of leads to her identification to the police in order to escape social censure. If she uses the role of a domestic for spying purposes, her connection with the crime may be so concealed that even apprehension of her male accomplices may leave her undetected. Thus, her participation in these two otherwise very reliably reported crimes is probably also underreported, and its real extent cannot be gathered to the same degree from criminal statistics as it can be for male offenders.

Larceny.

Woman's social roles give her many opportunities for theft. These opportunities, although very different in many respects, have one thing in common: they give the woman offender a chance to steal and remain undetected or at least unprosecuted to an extent which male thieves can never hope to enjoy. The pilfering domestic, the cunning pickpocket, the commercially valued, if errant, shopper, and the stealing prostitute all engage in types of larceny which—as will be seen below—have been rightly called secret theft and are excessively underreported in criminal statistics.[7]

Female pickpockets have received a considerable amount of attention, and the case material, as well as the general descriptions in the literature, demonstrates clearly in how many ways women offenders use the various roles of the female sex for concealment of their criminal attacks upon their victims' pockets. This characteristic element of their method of procedure is illustrated in the oldest case of a female pickpocket which has come to the attention of the writer. This was the case of an English woman in the early eighteenth century who with the help of a mechanical device feigned an advanced state of pregnancy and, seemingly struggling with her weakness in a pious effort to attend the Sunday services, rifled the pockets of her sympathetic neighbors in church.[8] The abuse of a specifically feminine role for criminal purposes, which is illustrated by the sham pregnancy of this woman, can also be recognized in other modi operandi of female pickpockets. There are sham prostitutes who use the pretense of soliciting as a cover for their attacks on the pockets of men. They try to perform the theft in the initial stages of conversation with the victims and sometimes prefer to get away without their purses or wallets rather than let the situation develop further along the lines suggested by their method of approach.[9] Then there are sham shoppers who operate in large department stores, usually in one which has a sale and thus can be expected to be crowded. They enter by the door farthest from the main entrance and work either in the elevators or on the upper floors, in order to avoid the store detectives, most of whom are stationed on the ground floor. Benefiting from the preoccupation of the shoppers who are either too crowded or too eager for a bargain to pay attention to their immediate surroundings, they open the bags of two or three women and, after having rifled them, stop their activities. This self-restraint is caused by their professional knowledge that after the discovery of two or three thefts the store detectives will be alerted and make further work difficult. There are said to be more female than male bag-openers, and the latter seem to refrain from working in department stores because a male shopper at a counter of ladies' goods usually attracts too much attention from the salesgirl, who expects him to buy more than a female shopper.[10] Another use of a feminine role is practiced by those women pickpockets who travel principally in buses and trolleys. Such an offender usually asks a man sitting beside her to open or close a window, then she goes through his pockets while he rises and concentrates his attention on his act of chivalry.[11]

The common characteristic of these various ways in which female pickpockets go about their trade is the deceptive use of a feminine role which throws the victim off his guard and facilitates the theft. How long some female pickpockets are able to work without detection can be well imagined and is illustrated by the fact that the notorious English pickpocket Elizabeth Thompson plied her trade for almost twelve months before she was caught for the first time. Thereafter, she continued to work again for years, averaging about $1,000 per month without being apprehended.[12]

Of course, male pickpockets also use methods of deceit in order to approach their victims, but their risk of discovery seems to be greater and their opportunities to work in certain localities fewer than the risk and opportunities of women pickpockets. It seems, therefore, that this crime, although never well reflected in criminal statistics, is particularly underreported if it is committed by women.

Theft by prostitutes from their customers is a universally observed phenomenon which has its roots in the social disapproval of these women and their ensuing association with criminal elements, with whom they join in their antagonism against society.[13] American, English, French, Spanish, Italian, and German authors have referred again and again to this type of theft and its extremely low prosecution. They have failed, however, to influence the statistical conclusions of most students of female crime.[14]

In many instances, the clients of a prostitute are under the influence of alcohol, and therefore easy prey of criminal attacks on their property. But even if they are sober, the prostitute has ways and means of getting at her customers. It has been described as a usual procedure that the girl at first only hides the object of her theft and does not concern herself with it until her visitor has left. If he should discover its disappearance, she encourages him to look for it, pretends to assist him in his search, and actually tries to guide him away from the place where it is hidden. If he nevertheless discovers it, she fakes great pleasure but asks to share in the recovered money either on account of having been "wrongly suspected" or as a remuneration for her "help" in finding it.[15]

Even in this specifically female crime, however, the woman may confine herself to the role of an accomplice, acting only as decoy, and leave the actual commission of the crime to a male partner. In such cases, the prostitute may suggest that her visitor put his coat on a chair by an open window in order to bring it within the reach of her male confederate. The latter bides his time until the attention of the victim is sufficiently diverted, and then reaches through the window from the outside and steals the wallet or watch of the victim.[16] If the prostitute has a poster bed with curtains, the chair may be in the middle of the room, and the male accomplice may enter through a panel door in the wall and go through the clothes of the victim, whose view is blocked by the curtain.[17]

It is obvious that the victim of such a theft will very rarely feel inclined to call the police into action. Fear of social disapproval of his sex conduct will in many instances deter him from any attempt to recover his property with the assistance of the law or to have the thief prosecuted, which would necessitate his appearance as a witness in court. The result of this situation is a great amount of unprosecuted crime. For instance, the prostitute Chicago May reports in her autobiography that she stole property from her clients almost daily; but her arrests on charges of theft during her whole career numbered about a dozen.[18]

Since the 1840's, shoplifting has been discussed as one of the most specifically female types of crime.[19] It has arisen out of the sales organization of the modern department store with its emphasis on the public's free examination of the goods and its occasionally permitted delay of contact with the sales personnel until the moment at which the customer wants to complete the purchase.[20] It is not confined to department stores, however, but occurs also at chain stores with self-service, and even in stores with a completely different sales organization, where articles of small size are sold.

Actually, it covers two different types of crime: the puzzling theft by the otherwise respectable woman and the depredations of the professional thief. It is particularly the former which by its unusual aspects has attracted a great deal of attention. The majority of the nonprofessional shoplifters are women of comfortable means who could buy the things they steal and who lead otherwise blameless lives.[21]

The objects most commonly stolen are pieces of dry goods, lingerie, cheap jewelry, or other objects which can be easily hidden and carried away.[22] They are usually of no apparent value to the offenders, who often have similar ones at home and sometimes to a far greater extent than necessary to satisfy their needs. Searches in their homes frequently bring to light considerable amounts of objects thus stolen, hidden in all possible places and with no signs of use, often still wearing the tags of the store from which they were taken.[23]

The divergence of the personality pattern of these shoplifters from the customary concept of the criminal has led many psychiatrists to explain this phenomenon by a special mental disease, kleptomania. They base their opinion on the fact that this type of misconduct, according to Healy's classic definition, is disproportionate to any discernible end in view.[24]

It has also led to a strong resistance on the part of the store managements to turn these unprofessional shoplifters over to the police. If the shopper is known to the store, it is often the practice simply to add the cost of the article to the bill. If she is not known, she is not disturbed until she is about to leave the store. Then she is asked to step "upstairs," where the matter is amicably settled.[25]

A number of authors report that the professional as well as the habitual shoplifters use special devices for the concealment of the objects which they steal. They work with special success in the winter season, when heavy pieces of outer wear facilitate the hiding of their loot. Sometimes special pockets are fitted into their garments for this purpose, thus making them real criminal equipment in the guise of women's clothes. The police have observed cases in which a shoplifter inserted into one sleeve of her coat an artificial arm. To the hand of that arm a bag was secured in order to give a more realistic appearance. Under this cover, she used her real hand for stealing.[26]

While the nonprofessional shoplifter works alone, the professionals work in pairs, one of them attracting the attention of the sales personnel and the other performing the theft. Sometimes the first one also takes the object and passes it on to the other, who has been careful not to come near the counter so that in case of discovery suspicion will not be directed at her but only at the first one, who by now can be searched without risk. It has also been reported that a favorite trick of professionals is to use the assistance of children. The woman shoplifter attracts the attention of the salesperson and at the same time holds her shopping bag open beneath the counter while the child knocks goods over the edge into the bag. If the behavior of the child should be noticed, the women gives him a maternal scolding and passes the incident off as a childish prank.[27]

In the instance of shoplifting, almost everything works against adequate representation among the larceny figures in criminal statistics. The basic pattern of concealment and its perfection in the cases of habituals and professionals, the insignificant value of the individual object of the theft, the social status of many offenders, and, most of all, the strong resistance by store managements to reporting nonprofessional shoplifters to the police, make this probably one of the least prosecuted offenses and one of the most underreported in criminal statistics.

Scientific interest in domestic thefts has been directed at the problem of causation rather than at the modus operandi; however, the literature contains some material which permits an extension of our investigation to this type of larceny. First, a distinction has to be made between the professional thief who uses domestic employment as an entering wedge in order to get access to private homes, and the real domestic who yields to the ever-present temptation to steal which household employment offers. The professional steals much and fast in order to finish the job. De Ryckère reports a considerable number of cases in which the professional committed the theft on her very first day of employment.[28] The more normal procedure seems to be that she tries first to gain the confidence of her employers by excellent performance of her duties, waits for the family's first extended absence, and then cleans out the place and leaves.[29]

The true domestic who falls into thievery does so usually after a period of faithful service. First, she yields to the temptation of the moment, but she may become a habitual offender, continuing in the employment and stealing only on occasion, or as a side line of her main job. If she steals only one object at a time she often avoids discovery, particularly by so timing her thefts that suspicion may fall on a craftsman, an electrician, or a plumber who was in the place at the critical period. The permanence of the opportunities offered to her by the nature of her employment makes it possible for her to steal summer things in the fall so that they are not missed during the winter, and winter things in the spring with a similar result. When the loss is discovered, the owner cannot remember when he last had the objects and where he put them, thus coming to the conclusion that they have been lost.[30]

Small thefts of food are not considered unlawful by many domestics. They consider them as customary in the profession, and it is just the smallness and material insignificance of the stolen objects which characterize the habitual domestic thief. This comparative insignificance of her thefts not only in her own but also in the eyes of her employer makes this offense not sufficiently injurious in public opinion to warrant much vigor in prosecution. The employee-employer relationship between her and her victim often leads to an inclination toward leniency on the part of the latter which makes dismissal rather than criminal prosecution the normal consequence of the discovery of the theft. Finally, her opportunity to bide her time in the committing of the offense often permits her to cover her tracks so successfully that no suspicion falls upon her. Thus, we have here a crime which at least in the case of the habitual offender lacks all three characteristics which are necessary for its adequate reflection in criminal statistics. It is true that the same quality can be found in the nonprofessional thefts of male domestics, but it must not be overlooked that the latter are only a minority among domestic workers. Again, we are faced with an offense which is in all probability very frequent and, in any case, more often committed by women than by men without being to any degree reliably reflected in criminal statistics.

Blackmail.

In the sphere of predatory crimes which are always greatly underreported, no matter whether the offender is a man or a woman, the female modus operandi suggests that women have numerous opportunities for criminal behavior which are not open to men. This is also an aspect of the female modus operandi which deserves the attention of the student of criminal statistics and can best—although by no means only—be demonstrated by an investigation of the ways in which women commit blackmail.

The threat to divulge damaging information about a person's past in order to extort money is used by male and female offenders alike.[31] It seems, however, that while men must find such information about the victim in the records of the past, women are able to actually create incidents which will furnish the necessary material. The protection of her sex honor which our society grants to woman and our disapproval of illicit sex conduct equip women blackmailers with a special weapon which they use either alone or in complicity with men, but which is not open to male blackmailers working alone.

First of all, there is the time-honored "husband" game. A man is invited by a woman to go with her to her place and, after having become established in a compromising situation, is surprised by footsteps and a noise outside. The woman is apparently terrified and tells the victim that this must be her husband whom she did not expect and who is certain to take a cruel revenge for the betrayal if he finds her with a visitor in such a situation. She seemingly tries to get the victim away, but it is too late. The "husband" enters, makes a terrible scene, and utters violent threats. In the course of his outburst, however, he makes the victim understand that money can buy his way out, and in many instances the latter accepts this suggestion.[32]

Similar is the work of the woman blackmailer who lets a man invite her for supper in a private room or receives him in her home, but then shows great indignation when the victim, encouraged by her behavior, makes any advances, and threatens to report him to the hotel manager or to the police unless he pays. This trick has been said to be a profitable side line, particularly of mannequins who work with traveling sales organizations and use the opportunities offered by their jobs to meet new victims.[33]

The opportunities of high-class prostitutes to blackmail wealthy clients can be easily visualized and are well illustrated in the already mentioned autobiography of Chicago May, whose recollections are invaluable for any student of the connection between prostitution and crime. The main problem in this type of blackmail is, of course, breaking the victim's incognito. To what length such prostitutes may go in their efforts to get at the identity of their visitors is indicated by the report that visitors who seemed promising enough have actually been shadowed for that reason.[34]

In some instances, the mere fact of illicit sex conduct does not seem to be an effective enough basis for blackmail to the woman offender, and pretended pregnancies and infections have been used for the purpose of getting money out of the victim. That real pregnancies and infections are similarly used needs hardly any elaboration.[35]

It must be concluded, therefore, that our sex mores offer female blackmailers opportunities which are not open to the male offender in this type of crime, and that this greater wealth of opportunities in all probability finds its reflection in the incidence of blackmail committed by women.

Fraud.

Edwin H. Sutherland's research on white-collar criminality has shown that fraudulent behavior contributes a great amount of unprosecuted crime committed by men, which formerly remained unnoticed. Study of female frauds suggests, however, that the undiscovered or at least unprosecuted criminality of women must be also very considerable for this offense.

Perhaps the most numerous group of female frauds is to be

found in the ranks of the domestics. It is well known that maids and particularly cooks often retain a small fraction of the money which their employers entrust to them for household purchases by misrepresenting the prices which they actually pay. In France, this profit is called *le sou du franc* and is so customary that the Gallic clergy recognized this practice as belonging to the behavior pattern of domestic service workers. In 1899 the Abbé Roby, professor of theology at the Seminary of St. Sulpice and moderator of the Commission of Conscience for the Archdiocese of Paris, advised the priests to show tolerance in this regard, if faced with confessions of this offense.[36] For the student of criminal statistics, it is again interesting to note that the sums involved in this type of fraud are so small that criminal action is hardly ever resorted to by the employer, even if the offense should be discovered.

Woman has always been a puzzle to man, and this aura of enigma has often led him to seek revelations from her which he would not expect from persons of his own sex. Established religions as well as superstitions have credited woman with the power to see in the future, and naturally enough women have used this credit given to their sex also in the field of crime. As late as in the nineteenth century, female astrologers and clairvoyants were reported as plying a considerable trade, and its existence can still be traced in the advertisement columns of the newspapers of that period. Large numbers of these female frauds are said to have made money out of the gullibility of people[37] and, although the better newspapers do not contain their advertisements any more, the offense of fortunetelling is still reported in recent publications and statistics.[38] Gypsy women particularly are still engaged in this questionable trade, capitalizing on the simple fact that everybody "wants to be loved, is interested in money, and has some worry or other."[39] The low fees usually asked by fortunetellers and the victims' feelings of shame over having consulted them make this a largely unprosecuted offense which, although insignificant in incidence, adds to the general picture of the masked character of female criminality.

That the cover of prostitution is used as a bait for the victim can be shown also for frauds. Chicago May reports a practice whereby girls solicit men ostensibly for immoral purposes, insist on advance payment, and then lure them into certain hotels where there is no water in the rooms. Pretending that they are going for water, they get out of the room and never return. Men who are so cheated are called "Johns," and Chicago May recalls in her memoirs that often she had as many as ten "Johns" per night.[40]

Women have also been reported as accomplices of male crooks in horse-racing tricks. They are usually very attractive, inveigle middle-aged men by their charms, and pretend to be completely unacquainted with the practices of the race track. After having gained the confidence of the victim by flawless behavior for a couple of weeks, they use the opportunity of their being taken along to the races to tell the victim of a dream which suggests a winner and express the desire to test the dream by betting on a particular horse. This story usually produces a generous sum from their indulgent "protector." If the horse wins, and it is usually a good "tip," the woman tells the victim that she has by mistake put the money on another horse, shows great distress, and produces a faked betting slip. The victim frequently comforts her for the pretended loss with another present, and in the meantime her male accomplices collect the money. If the horse loses, the trick is repeated until it works. The whole trick is nothing but gambling with somebody else's money.[41]

Another type of fraud in which female accomplices are used is the disposition of fake jewelry by the professional pawner. The faker usually buys a quantity of rolled gold trinkets and works a small piece of genuine gold into each. The woman helper takes the product to a pawnbroker and offers it for what it may be worth, making no statement as to its being real gold. The pawnbroker tests it by acid application and, if he happens to hit the piece of real gold, buys the whole trinket as such. If he hits another spot, he refuses to buy. According to the law of probability, the woman tries other pawnbrokers until she has disposed of the whole stock.[42]

In summary, it can be said that women offenders in the field

of fraud engage in a number of activities which hardly ever lead
to the coöperation of the victim with the police and which are
not open to male offenders because they represent the abuse of
opportunities offered by specifically feminine social roles.

NOTES

1 Edith R. Spaulding, "The Value of Mental, Physical and Social Studies of
Delinquent Women," *Journal of the American Institute of Criminal Law and
Criminology*, IX (1918-19), 92; The Committee on Criminal Courts of the
Charity Organization Society of the City of New York, *The Adolescent
Offender*, p. 47; Franz Exner, *Krieg und Kriminalität in Österreich*, p. 153;
Hans Schneickert, "Das Weib als Erpresserin und Anstifterin," *Abhandlungen
aus dem Gebiete der Sexualforschung*, I (1918-19), 9.

2 Lucas, *op. cit.*, pp. 89-90.

3 George Ellington, *The Women of New York*, p. 500; William Douglas
Morrison, *Crime and Its Causes*, p. 153; Ashton-Wolfe, *op. cit.*, pp. 249-50;
De Ryckère, *La Servante Criminelle*, p. 106.

4 Bishop, *Women and Crime*, pp. 10-11.

5 Schneickert, *op. cit.*, p. 9; Franz Exner, *Krieg und Kriminalität in
Österreich*, p. 156.

6 Ashton-Wolfe, *op. cit.*, pp. 252-53.

7 Farley, *op. cit.*, p. 206; Devon, *op. cit.*, p. 144; Schneickert, *op. cit.*, p. 9;
Antheaume, *op. cit.*, pp. 23-24.

8 Pike, *op. cit.*, p. 279.

9 J. Sanderson Christison, *Crime and Criminals*, pp. 56-59; Devon, *op. cit.*,
p. 145; Bishop, *From Information Received*, pp. 163-65.

10 Harry Söderman and John J. O'Connell, *Modern Criminal Investigation*,
10th printing, pp. 343-44.

11 Ellington, *op. cit.*, p. 442.

12 Farley, *op. cit.*, pp. 509-10.

13 Iwan Bloch and Georg Loewenstein, *Die Prostitution*, II-1, p. 222.

14 Sellin, "The Basis of a Crime Index," p. 339; Gladys Mary Hall, *Prostitu-
tion in the Modern World*, p. 43; Devon, *op. cit.*, p. 145; Bishop, *Women and
Crime*, p. 56; Granier, *op. cit.*, pp. 257-58; Lombroso and Ferrero, *op. cit.*,
p. 543; C. Bernaldo de Quirós and J. M. L. Aguilaniedo, *Verbrechertum und
Prostitution in Madrid*, p. 132; Käte Schmitz, *Die Kriminalität der Frau*, p. 43.
Frank J. Curran, "Specific Trends in Criminality of Women," *Journal of
Criminal Psychopathology*, III (1941-42), 617-18, 623.

15 Granier, *op. cit.*, p. 266.

16 Hall, *op. cit.*, p. 44.

17 Ellington, *op. cit.*, p. 204.

18 Sellin, "The Basis of a Crime Index," p. 339; Devon, *op. cit.*, p. 145; Otto
Mönkemöller, *Korrektionsanstalt und Landarmenhaus, Ein soziologischer
Beitrag zur Kriminalität und Psychopathologie des Weibes*, pp. 49-51; May
Churchill Sharpe, *Chicago May*, p. 46; Schmitz, *op. cit.*, p. 43.

19 De Greeff, *op. cit.*, p. 249.

20 Paul Dubuisson, "Les Voleuses des Grands Magasins," *Archives D'Anthropologie Criminelle*, XVI (1901), 17.

21 Granier, *op. cit.*, pp. 247-48; The Committee on Criminal Courts of the
Charity Organization Society of the City of New York, *op. cit.*, p. 64.

22 Thomas Byrnes (Inspector Byrnes), *Professional Criminals of America*, pp. 30-32; Farley, *op. cit.*, p. 53.

23 Healy, *op. cit.*, p. 771; Locard, *op. cit.*, p. 52.

24 Healy, *op. cit.*, p. 771; Eugen Bleuler, *Textbook of Psychiatry*, authorized English ed. by A. A. Brill, p. 539; D. K. Henderson and R. D. Gillespie, *A Textbook of Psychiatry for Students and Practitioners*, fifth ed., p. 313; and many others.

25 J. P. Shalloo, *Private Police, With Special Reference to Pennsylvania*, pp. 194-95.

26 Goodwin, *op. cit.*, p. 56; Farley, *op. cit.*, pp. 53-54; Ellington, *op. cit.*, p. 447; Söderman and O'Connell, *op. cit.*, p. 335; Antheaume, *op. cit.*, p. 24; Emil Raimann, "Über Warenhausdiebinnen," *Monatsschrift für Kriminalpsychologie und Strafrechtsreform*, XIII (1922), 315.

27 Byrnes, *op. cit.*, p. 31; Bishop, *Women and Crime*, pp. 7-8.

28 De Ryckère, *La Servante Criminelle*, pp. 76 ff.

29 Söderman and O'Connell, *op. cit.*, p. 334.

30 *Ibid.*, pp. 333-34; De Ryckère, *La Servante Criminelle*, p. 71.

31 Ashton-Wolfe, *op. cit.*, p. 256.

32 Ellington, *op. cit.*, pp. 205-6; Barnes and Teeters, *op. cit.*, p. 570.

33 Bishop, *Women and Crime*, p. 205.

34 Sharpe, *op. cit.*, p. 87.

35 Schneickert, *op. cit.*, pp. 10-12.

36 De Ryckère, *La Servante Criminelle*, p. 67.

37 Ellington, *op. cit.*, pp. 412-36.

38 Schmitz, *op. cit.*, p. 62; City of New York, *Annual Report of the Police Department for 1940*, p. 136; Wullfen, *op. cit.*, p. 105.

39 Arlene Helen Bonos, "Roumany Rye of Philadelphia," *American Anthropologist*, XLIV, New Series (1942), 271.

40 Sharpe, *op. cit.*, p. 35.

41 Bishop, *From Information Received*, p. 71.

42 Goodwin, *op. cit.*, p. 28.

CHAPTER V

THE REAL EXTENT OF FEMALE CRIME

The material presented in the preceding chapters has strongly suggested that the crimes of women remain underreported to a greater extent than do the crimes of men. The literature contains, however, still more tangible evidence to this effect, and the presentation of this material must now follow as the next step in our analysis.

Of course, undiscovered crime is beyond the reach of any quantitative assessment. However, many offenses which are committed by women are underreported only because they remain unprosecuted, and attempts to estimate or even to measure the incidence of some of these latter offenses have been made. Research efforts of this type have been directed particularly at criminal abortions and thefts in department stores.

If there is any one offense which occurs in tremendous volume but is practically unprosecuted, it is criminal abortion. Medical literature contains an abundance of evidence to this effect. The sum total of all abortions has been estimated repeatedly for the United States and other countries, and the percentages of these totals which are composed of criminal abortions have also been made an object of research. These estimates—although by no means agreed upon by the experts—throw an interesting light on the real extent of this offense for which the woman involved is frequently responsible under positive statutory regulations. Since this is not a legal treatise, the question whether or not under common law the woman who submits to an abortion is a participant in its commission or even a principal under the rules regulating aiding and abetting may be left within the realm of controversy.[1] But no such controversy regarding the criminal character of her behavior can exist in states which, like New York and California, make it a special statutory offense to submit to an abortion or to perform one upon oneself.[2] In France, similarly, no such question can arise because there the criminal responsibility of the woman submitting to an abortion is expressly stated in the criminal code. In Germany it is court practice to consider the woman who submits to an abortion criminally responsible.[3] In view of this legal situation, it is important to realize that even the lowest estimates of criminal abortions suggest female crime figures which would greatly affect our traditional notion about the incidence of female crime and even more so those about the quantitative sex differential in crime.

The estimates of the yearly number of abortions in the United States vary greatly; they have been set at 333,000, 350,000, 600,000, 700,000, 1,000,000, and 2,000,000.[4] The estimates of the percentage composed of criminal abortions also vary considerably, giving figures of 30 per cent, between 33 per cent and 66 per cent, and 95 per cent.[5] If we accept the authority of Taussig, whose book on abortion is considered a classic in this field, for a total of about 700,000 cases per year and the minimum estimate of 30 per cent for criminal abortions, we arrive at a seemingly conservative estimate of 210,000 interruptions of pregnancy which constitute criminal offenses on the part of the abortionist. To be sure, not all these cases may implicate the woman who underwent the abortion as a criminal offense, because in many states she would not be held responsible for complicity with the abortionist. However, as previously indicated, at least in New York and California she would be responsible for a specific offense. It is interesting to note that hardly any prosecutions for this offense seem to occur in either of these two states. The best illustration of the degree to which the criminal behavior of the abortee herself is disregarded by our law-enforcing agencies can be found in the proceedings against the Pacific Coast Abortion Ring which aroused considerable interest in the thirties. Rankin, the head of this large-scale organization of abortionists, boasted that his outfit handled 4,400 cases during the years of its existence, and the patient records found in the various offices of the organization filled several large canvas sacks. Not one of the women who had engaged the services of this organization seems to have been prosecuted, however.[6]

The situation in France seems to be even worse, and its criminal aspects have received repeated attention.[7] Pre-war estimates for that country vary between 300,000 and 400,000 abortions yearly,[8] which, considering the population base of about 40,000,000, is considerably higher than the more conservative estimates for the United States. Against the background of a total of between 300,000 and 400,000 abortions, there were about 400 accusations yearly, and only a fraction of those led to convictions as the figures of 158 convictions for 1933 and of 143 convictions for 1934 suggest.[9] It is interesting to note that the French experts seem to consider the total abortion figures as composed of criminal abortions only, and that they seem to be more concerned about their being probably too low than about their comprising also therapeutic cases. Whether this is to be interpreted as a case of negligence or as an expression of the greater realism of the French must be left to the judgment of the reader.

The German authors of the pre-Nazi period viewed the abortion situation in their country in a similar light and were on occasions rather emphatic in denouncing the mock picture offered by the conviction figures contained in criminal statistics.[10] Before World War I, abortions in Germany were estimated to amount to between 9 per cent and 10 per cent of all pregnancies. After that war, the percentage was estimated to be about 30 per cent and in some urban centers such as Berlin, and Dortmund even 40 per cent. Assuming criminal and therapeutic abortions to represent on the average only 30 per cent of all pregnancies, a German expert estimated that in consideration of the occurrence of 1,600,000 births in 1923 the yearly incidence of criminal abortions in Germany amounted to 400,000 cases at that time.[11] Against this figure, the German criminal statistics for 1923 listed 3,565 convictions for criminal abortions or not quite 1 for every 100 cases.[12]

Data of a similar nature could be easily produced for other countries, but this seems unnecessary because the figures presented for the United States, France, and Germany show beyond any doubt that the consideration of criminal abortions as a part of the real criminality of women would add large amounts of crime to the reported numbers of female offenses in any one country. The estimates of the incidence of criminal abortions are not as yet reliable enough and sufficiently agreed upon by the experts to justify a numerical calculation of the real extent of female crime in this respect, but a statistical experiment may show the potential fruitfulness of further research along these lines.

If we accept the conservative estimate of 210,000 criminal abortions yearly for the United States as presented above and assume that the proportionate figure for New York State would be 1/10, or 21,000 cases, the addition of the offense figures derived from this crime to the male and female offenses known to the police and leading to arrest in New York State would effect remarkable changes in the sex differential apparent in the police statistics of this state. For 1940, for instance, the Commissioner of Correction reported 331,062 male and 29,020 female arrests, or a sex differential of 11.4 male to 1 female arrest.[13] Before adding the corresponding criminal abortion figures, we have to consider that in the majority of abortions the sex partner of the abortee is an accessory to the crime at least by paying the bill of the abortionist. It seems that only in cases of self-induced abortions men do not enter the picture to any noticeable degree. While thus in the majority of cases the offense will at least implicate one woman and one man beside the abortionist, the latter type of abortion will probably implicate the woman offender alone. One of the most comprehensive studies of birth control practices now permits an estimate of the proportion of self-induced cases to the total composed of all types of criminal abortions. In her study of 10,000 case histories of the Birth Control Clinical Research Bureau in New York City, Marie E. Kopp found 1,863 self-induced cases in a total of 7,667 criminal abortions, or a proportion of 24 per cent.[14] Her sample was in all probability biased with regard to this particular question because the incidence of women who resort to self-induced abortion may well be higher in population groups which have no access to birth control clinics. We are, therefore, probably conservative in accepting this percentage as representative of the part which self-induced abortions play in the whole of New York State. Still 24 per cent of 21,000 assumed criminal abortions would give us 5,040 cases in which men are probably not implicated as parties to the offense. We would, therefore, have to add the cases of 21,000 abortees but only the 15,960 offenses of male parties to the crime to the respective groups of arrest. This would let us arrive at new totals of 347,022 male and of 50,020 female offenses for New York State, or at a sex ratio of 6.9 male per 1 female offense, if we accept the inaccuracy implied in taking arrest figures as reflecting the incidence of offenses, which at the present state of arrest statistics cannot be avoided. This calculation would still omit the offenses committed by the abortionists, among whom midwives figure to a considerable degree. Even without the further increase in male and female crime resulting from that source, the limited inclusion of the incidence of only this one generally unprosecuted crime would change the sex ratio of 11.4 male per 1 female offense to 6.9 male per 1 female offense.

Equally interesting regarding the real extent of female crime are the reports on shoplifting contained in the American, English, and French literature. It has already been indicated at an earlier point of this investigation that it is a policy in department stores to avoid court proceedings against shoplifters who are not professionals,[15] but to what extent this policy prevents the prosecution of female crime deserves further examination.

In his *Memorandum on Crime in the Depression,* Sellin reports the results of an inquiry into shoplifting in three large Philadelphia department stores which are perhaps the most telling indictment of the coverage of this type of larceny by official criminal statistics so far published in the literature. This inquiry covers the store experience over a period of six years and shows separate figures for thefts known to the stores, thefts which led to arrest by the store police, and thefts which led to official prosecution and conviction. It permits, furthermore, a comparison of the thefts known to the stores with the whole number of thefts known to the Philadelphia police in the corresponding years. The figures presented in the following table gain increased significance by the fact that one department store in Philadelphia, about equal in size to the three stores studied, and several smaller ones were not included in the investigation.

TABLE 3
SHOPLIFTING IN THREE PHILADELPHIA STORES, 1928-33*

Year	Thefts Known to Stores	Arrests by Store Detectives	Prosecuted and Convicted	Thefts Known to Police[a]
1928	4,935	1,147	227	6,318
1929	4,828	1,035	223	6,429
1930	5,172	1,077	252	7,505
1931	5,381	1,180	226	7,088
1932	5,277	1,267	253	5,604
1933	5,314	1,432	230	4,402
Average	5,151	1,190	235	6,224

* Based on Sellin, *Research Memorandum on Crime in the Depression,* p. 69.
  [a] This includes data for the entire city except the number of persons "Prosecuted and Convicted." They should be added to get the official totals recorded by the city police.

The average figure of 5,151 thefts known to these three stores per year suggests a weekly number of about 33 thefts per store, the average yearly figure of 1,190 arrests made by the store detectives a weekly store average of 7 shoplifters caught, and the average number of prosecutions and convictions a proportion of only 4.6 per cent of the known volume of these offenses.

These Philadelphia figures find a simile in Cecil Bishop's estimates of the incidence and prosecution of English shoplifters about 1930. According to him, the average number of shoplifters caught in the large department stores in London was about 20 per week. The losses resulting from shoplifting averaged yearly between £15,000 and £20,000 per store. The reluctance of the store managements to prosecute shoplifters was mainly due to the loss of work which would have resulted from the time which the store employees would have had to spend as witnesses in court and which Bishop estimated would have amounted to 4,160 work days per year for a store with the average weekly 20 arrests, if the management should have decided to have all shoplifters charged who were caught. Finally, Bishop estimated that the women charged with shoplifting in England did not even represent fully 2 per cent of those who pilfered.[16]

It seems that even these startling figures are, however, far surpassed by the reports of the large department stores in Paris.

According to Antheaume, the Louvre informed him in the course of his research on kleptomania that they observed 20 thefts daily, the Galeries Lafayette reported 8-10 daily thefts, and the Printemps 10. The Louvre and the Galeries Lafayette reported also that their managements in almost all cases gave the *désistement,* the declaration not to prosecute. The other department stores in Paris investigated by Antheaume gave lower figures, but explained that they preferred to prevent a disturbance in their public relations to catching a shoplifter to whom it was difficult to deny the *désistement.* On the basis of this investigation, Antheaume concluded that the daily average of thefts in nine large department stores in Paris was about 100 and the yearly average because of Sundays and holidays 30,000.[17]

That the business policies prevailing in large chain stores work in a similar direction of leaving shoplifters unprosecuted can be gathered by the following procedure reported in a professional sales periodical. According to this publication, a chain of supermarkets tries to retain the good will of its errant customers by purposeful leniency in its dealings with shoplifters. If shortages in a branch become disturbingly great and cannot be traced to any other reason, a special investigator is sent to watch for pilferers from the counters. A person who has been detected as a shoplifter is approached on the street and invited to come back and see the manager of the market. The latter explains to the shoplifter that there is a choice between two alternatives: either to confess or to undergo arrest by the police. The manager then continues that the store has no desire to prosecute and prefers to settle the matter quietly with the customer. He asks the shoplifter for identification and then produces a confession blank, which he explains will not be used against the culprit unless the store discovers a repetition of the offense. The shoplifter almost always signs, and the confession is then forwarded to headquarters where it is kept in a confidential file. The manager, before releasing the shoplifter, takes care to explain that the store is interested in keeping its customers and that regret over the unfortunate incident can best be shown by continued patronage.[18] From the point of view of the statistician, it is interesting to note that according to the same report a special investigator averages about 20 apprehensions per week. Of course, he is sent only to markets where the situation is considered grave; the mere fact, however, that chain stores have such special employees on their staff together with the number of food markets with self-service in this country suggests that the number of thefts committed in these stores and not reported because of such policies must be of impressive size.

It seems unnecessary to proceed with further evidence. The figures from Philadelphia and Paris and the estimates from London regarding shoplifters in department stores, as well as the reported prosecution policy in chain stores, leave little doubt that the relationship between prosecution and incidence of shoplifting is so remote that no reliance whatsoever can be placed on criminal statistics in an effort to gauge the real extent of this largely female type of larceny. Actually, the quantitative research regarding the real extent of shoplifting and its relation to the figures presented in police statistics is much more tangible than the estimates regarding the incidence of criminal abortions. It may be permissible, therefore, to make also a statistical experiment of assessing the influence of a consideration of the probable incidence of this type of crime on the sex differential apparent in criminal statistics.

The Philadelphia figures produced by Sellin indicate that in 1933 there were more cases of shoplifting known to only three department stores than all the thefts known to the police for the whole of Philadelphia.[19] Taken over the six-year average, 1928-33, the cases known to the three stores equaled 80 per cent of the number of the thefts known to the police for all of the city. Considering the fact that not even half of the Philadelphia department stores and not one chain store were covered by this study, it may not be too much to say that the total volume of shoplifting going on in the city is double the amount of all thefts known to the police. If we transpose this assumption to New York City, which because of the amount and the size of its department and chain store organizations is again a very conservative procedure, we would have to assume that the actual amount of shoplifting in that city is also at least double the amount of the whole volume of thefts known to the police. In the year 1940, the New York City police made 2,219 male and 705 female arrests for petty larceny, and 121,961 male and 12,296 female arrests for all types of offenses.[20] The sex ratio according to male and female arrests was, therefore, 3 male for 1 female case of petty theft and 10 male for 1 female case in general. According to Sutherland, the percentage of male to female shoplifters apprehended in a Chicago department store suggested that 70 per cent of all persons caught in committing this offense are women.[21] If we assume this to be representative also for New York, we would have to add 30 per cent of double the amount of all petty larcenies known to the New York City police to the male figures, and 70 per cent of this number to the female figures, for this offense. The whole volume of petty larcenies reported for New York City in 1940 was 2,924. Double the amount, or 5,848, would correspond to the minimum figure of shoplifting which Sellin's research would suggest to have actually occurred. Thirty per cent of this figure, or 1,754, would have to be added to the 2,219 male arrests for petty theft listed in the police statistics. Seventy per cent of it, or 4,094, would have to be added to the 705 female arrests for the same offense. This calculation would result in 3,973 male and 4,799 female petty larceny cases in New York City for the year 1940, and the sex differential for this offense would immediately suggest a preponderance of women offenders. But even the sex ratio of arrests for all offenses would be seriously affected by this consideration of the probable extent of female and male shoplifting. The 121,961 male arrests for all offenses covered by the police increased by 1,754 male cases of shoplifting which were not listed in the arrest statistics of the police would give a total figure of 123,715 male offenses. The 12,296 female arrests for all offenses covered by the police increased by 4,094 female cases of shoplifting not listed in the arrest statistics of the police would give a total of 16,390 female offenses, and the sex ratio would be changed from 10 male for 1 female case to 7.5 male for 1 female case. Again, it must be stressed that these changes would be produced by the consideration of only one largely unprosecuted offense.[22]

After having shown in two instances what the inclusion of the conservative estimates of only one of the greatly underreported crimes would do to the sex differential apparent in criminal statistics, it seems desirable to attempt a showing of the probable cumulative effect of the inclusion of at least both of the offenses so far considered, namely criminal abortions and shoplifting. If, in order to keep the New York City situation as an example, we should transpose the abortion estimates for New York State to New York City and add the so derived figures to the official arrest figures plus the estimated figures on shoplifting, we would obtain the following picture. The 1940 Census gave 13,479,142 people for the whole state and 7,454,995 for New York City.[23] This shows the city of New York to comprise 55 per cent of the whole population of the state. If we disregard the observation that cities usually show a relatively strong contingent of young unmarried women and assume that the abortion figures for the whole state, although lower, are representative of New York City (which is probably erring on the conservative side) we would have to add 55 per cent of the 15,960 estimated male accessories, or 8,778 male cases, to the male arrests in New York City and 55 per cent of the estimated 21,000 abortees, or 11,550 additional cases, to the female arrests listed by the police of that city. These, together with the estimated sex groups of shoplifters not covered by the police statistics, would result in the following composite picture:

TABLE 4

SEX GROUPS OF ARRESTS IN NEW YORK CITY, 1940,
CORRECTED FOR CRIMINAL ABORTIONS AND SHOPLIFTING

Male arrests apparent in police statistics	121,961	Female arrests apparent in police statistics	12,296
Estimated male cases of shoplifting not listed under above	1,754	Estimated female cases of shoplifting not listed under above	4,094
Estimated number of male parties to criminal abortion not listed under above	8,778	Estimated number of abortees not listed under above	11,550
		Total	27,940
Total	132,493		

The new totals arrived at in this fashion present a sex ratio of 4.7 male for 1 female case. In other words, the inclusion of the probable numbers of male and female offenses in these two types of crime would already change the apparent sex ratio from 10 male offenses per 1 female offense to 4.7 male offenses per 1 female offense, and abortions and shoplifting are by no means the only greatly underreported offenses in which women take an outstanding part.

We cannot, however, rest our argument for the untenability of our traditional beliefs in the quantitative sex differential in crime with these considerations. The question has still to be examined whether male crime is not also underreported to such an extent that the inclusion of male as well as female unreported crime would restore the apparent sex differential. That this does not seem to be the case appears from the following considerations.

First of all, it must be kept in mind that the inclusion of those largely underreported crimes in which men and women take an equal part would add only equal numbers of male and female criminals to the known numbers of the respective offender groups. Because of the much lower number of the female offenders apparent in criminal statistics, however, such an addition must already bring the differential down. This consequence of simple mathematics can be easily demonstrated by the assumption of a male offender group of 100 and a female offender group of 10 representing a sex ratio of 10 to 1. Addition of equal numbers of 100 to both offender groups would give 200 male offenders and 110 female offenders, or a sex ratio of 1.8 to 1. The working of this law has already been shown in refined form in the two statistical experiments presented above.

It is now interesting to consider that the perhaps largest unprosecuted male offender group, the white-collar criminals, belong to a social stratum which employs one of the largest groups of female unprosecuted offenders which we have been able to discover, namely, the female domestic workers who by their thefts and frauds in all probability match in numbers, although not in social harmfulness, the more lucrative crimes of their employers. Another excessively underreported offense, adultery, comprises in every act the same number of man and woman offenders, so that its inclusion in an assessment of the real extent of male and female crime would have only the effect of bringing the apparent sex ratio down.

The inclusion of the one male offender group which seems to be really favored by laxity in law enforcement,[24] the men who engage in illicit sex conduct with prostitutes, would not change this situation. First of all, it must be understood that the crime of prostitution as such can be committed only by women because of the statutory definition of this behavior.[25] The male customer of the prostitute is not a party to the offense of prostitution. It is also held that resorting to a house of ill fame for an isolated act of intercourse does not constitute open and gross lewdness.[26] The man makes himself guilty only of such crimes as fornication or adultery. Fornication and adultery, however, are offenses in which the woman, in addition to the offense of prostitution, becomes also implicated in every act of her professional activities, because the act of illicit sex conduct must be distinguished from the act of offering one's body for indiscriminate intercourse with men. The behavior of the prostitute includes, therefore, two parts in every instance of her activities, the offering of her services in the sense of prostitution and the illicit sex behavior in the sense of fornication or adultery. Thus, if the criminal behavior of the male customer should be included in the consideration of the actual crime volume of the sexes, the same would have to be done for the corresponding criminal behavior on the part of the prostitute. This would do no more than add just another equal number of male and female offenses to the recorded amount of crime. The consequences of such a procedure for the quantitative sex differential in crime, however, have already been discussed.

Furthermore, it must be considered that prostitution as such goes largely unprosecuted also. It has been estimated that before World War I there were about 200,000 prostitutes in the United States.[27] In view of the increase of our population and the moral backwash of World War II, there is hardly any reason to assume that these figures have gone down. Still, only 5,816 female arrests for prostitution and commercialized vice were reported by the Uniform Crime Reports for 1947.[28] It is obvious that any serious consideration of the actual cases of soliciting which 200,000 prostitutes must commit per year would make this arrest number dwindle into insignificance. Actually, such a consideration alone would throw all impressions of a higher male crime volume out of gear, because we would have to consider millions of individual

offenses committed by women for which there is no male coun-
terpart—those cases in which the offer of a prostitute is not
accepted.

If we then further visualize the amount of undetected female
homicides, of undetected female accomplices of apprehended
male criminals, the unprosecuted crimes of prostitutes because
of the noncoöperation of the victims with the police, the opportunities for blackmail resulting from the sex mores of our culture,
the complete disregard of female homosexuality and of the sex
offenses of women committed on children under the cover of
child care, their undiscovered wrong accusations against men
which land the victims in jail and let the women offenders go
free, we have little choice but to accept the conclusion that the
numerical sex differential in crime as visualized in the past is a
myth. This myth has resulted from the temptation to accept the
surface impression furnished by official crime statistics without
further probing and a complete disregard of all the cautions
indicated by the work of Ferri and Sellin for their analysis. In
summary, we have overlooked the fact that our mores and folk-
ways have kept, and still largely keep, women at home or otherwise protected, and in consequence their crimes are under cover
to a much greater degree than is the case with men. That, with
such a bias in our search, our findings regarding the criminality
of women have been misleading is not surprising.

NOTES

1 See 1 *Corpus Juris Secundum*, 323-24.

2 *Penal Law of New York*, Art. 6 §81 (McKinney's 1944); *Penal Code of the
State of California*, §275 (Deering 1931).

3 *Code Pénal*, Art. 317; *Das Reichs-Strafgesetzbuch*, §218 (Ebermayer, Eichel-
baum, Lobe, Rosenberg, 1920).

4 National Committee on Maternal Health, Inc., *The Abortion Problem*,
pp. 10, 23; Scott C. Runnels, "Criminal Abortions as a Public Health
Problem," *The Journal of the American Institute of Homeopathy*, XXXIII
(1940), 491; Frederick J. Taussig, *Abortion Spontaneous and Induced*, p. 26;
Raymond E. Watkins, "A Five-Year Study of Abortion," *American Journal of
Obstetrics and Gynecology*, XXVI (1933), 161; Max Sylvius Handman, "Abortion," *Encyclopaedia of the Social Sciences*, I (1930), 373; A. J. Rongy, *Abortion: Legal or Illegal?*, p. 89.

5 Lucius E. Burch, "Treatment of Abortion," *Journal of the Tennessee State
Medical Association*, XXI (1928-29), 172; Maine Medical Association, Com-

mittee on Maternal and Child Welfare, "Abortion," *The Journal of the Maine Medical Association*, XXXIV (1943), 72; Rongy, *op. cit.*, p. 89.

6 Charles B. Pinkham, "The Pacific Coast Abortion Ring," *Federation Bulletin*, XXIII (1937), 48 ff.

7 A. Lacassagne, *Peine de Mort et Criminalité*, pp. 81-86; Jacques Bertillon, *La Dépopulation de la France*, pp. 241-45; M. Balthazard, "Quarante années de lutte contre l'avortement," *Annales de Médecine Légale*, XXII (1942), 102; Société de Médecine Légale de France, "Rapport de la Commission Chargée d'Étudier les Questions concernant l'Avortement et la Dénatalité (B. Desplas, Rapporteur)," *Annales de Médecine Légale*, XIX (1939), 539.

8 Balthazard, *op. cit.*, p. 102; "Rapport de la Commission Chargée d'Étudier les Questions concernant l'Avortement et la Dénatalité," p. 539.

9 "Rapport de la Commission Chargée d'Étudier les Questions concernant l'Avortement et la Dénatalité," p. 539.

10 Aschaffenburg, *op. cit.*, pp. 9, 158; Moritz Liepmann, *Krieg und Kriminalität in Deutschland*, p. 153.

11 Lönne, "Über die Zunahme der Fruchtabtreibungen vom Standpunkt der Volksgesundheit und Rassenhygiene," Kleinere Mitteilungen, *Archiv für Kriminologie*, LXXX (1927), 59.

12 Liepmann, *op. cit.*, p. 153.

13 State of New York, *Eleventh Annual Report of the Commissioner of Correction on Crime Statistics*, p. 158.

14 Marie E. Kopp, *Birth Control in Practice*, Appendix Table XXII.

15 See Chapter IV, p. 35.

16 Bishop, *Women and Crime*, pp. 6-8.

17 Antheaume, *op. cit.*, pp. 140-53.

18 Joseph A. Fletcher, "Shoplifting Can Be Licked," *Chainstore Age* (Grocery Executive Ed.), December 1940, pp. 30, 50-54.

19 See Table 3 of this chapter.

20 State of New York, *Eleventh Annual Report of the Commissioner of Correction on Crime Statistics*, p. 173.

21 Sutherland, *op. cit.*, 3rd ed., p. 100.

22 For the official arrest figures underlying this calculation see: *State of New York, Eleventh Annual Report of the Commissioner of Correction on Crime Statistics*, p. 173.

23 Sixteenth Census of the United States, *Population*, II, Part 5, pp. 13, 156.

24 Sutherland, *op. cit.*, 3rd ed., p. 101; Wood and Waite, *op. cit.*, p. 237; Eugenia C. Lekkerkerker, *Reformatories for Women in the United States*, p. 28.

25 42 *American Jurisprudence* 260.

26 33 *American Jurisprudence* 17.

27 Howard B. Woolston, *Prostitution in the United States*, I, p. 38.

28 *Uniform Crime Reports*, Vol. XVIII (1947), No. 2, p. 115.

CHAPTER VI

SOCIAL EMANCIPATION AND INCREASE OF FEMALE CRIME

In the preceding chapters it has been shown that the real amount of female crime is far greater than has generally been assumed. Continuing in our investigation, we now must ask whether this volume of crime is increasing, stationary, or decreasing.

The question of the quantitative movement of the criminality of women in the course of time has been the subject of a controversy of long standing. Ever since the 1870's, criminologists have predicted that the progressing social equalization between the sexes and particularly the entrance of women into ever wider fields of economic pursuits would lead to an increase in the volume of female crime and thereby to a decrease, if not a disappearance, of the sex differential apparent in criminal statistics.[1] Others, however, among them Aschaffenburg and Georg von Mayr, have denied any such consequence of this social trend and have presented statistics in support of their contention.[2]

It was certainly a weakness of both the proponents and the opponents of this hypothesis that they accepted the quantitative sex differential so misleadingly suggested by criminal statistics as at least basically valid. It must not be overlooked, however, that the quantitative movement of female crime in its relation to the changing position of woman in our society is of great research interest, no matter what the relationship between the extent of male and female criminality may actually be. An analysis of the available material is therefore indicated.

Before this material is presented in detail, a few general considerations are necessary. Every investigation of the female crime rate is, first of all, faced with the question whether criminal statistics are adequate research tools for gauging the changes which the real criminality of women may undergo with the years. In this connection one difficulty need not concern us. The difference between the sexes in the coverage of crime by official statistics is no obstacle in an investigation which confines itself to an assessment of changes in female criminality only. However, index questions are to be considered, and the number of difficulties in this respect is unfortunately very great. It has been seen already how invariably all types of crime which are normally used for index purposes lose their index quality if they are committed by women. It has furthermore to be considered that long-time trends concerning the incidence of crime cannot be worked out for a number of reasons. The data which are available for the longest periods back refer to numbers of prisoners[3] and are, therefore, by their very nature almost without index value.[4] Even if we reduced the stretch of time to be covered in order to get arrest data, or at least conviction figures, we would not have gained much. The value of that material would still be impaired by the changes which occur in prosecution policy, methods of reporting, and the substantive criminal law over periods of time. If we then finally limit ourselves to periods for which such variables can be discounted, we shall have achieved the comparability of data at the price of getting spot evidence which does not furnish a sufficient basis for the claim of general validity.[5] And still another difficulty has to be considered. Much of the material used in the previous investigations of this question refers only to general crime rates, which again are of only very limited index quality.[6]

Besides difficulties arising from the nature of criminal statistics at their present stage of development, there are others which stem from a neglect of the differences in the tempo of woman's emancipation at various periods in different countries. Obviously, international statistical comparisons which are undertaken without consideration of time lags in this social development will produce apparently contradictory data. Furthermore, some authors have considered social equalization between the sexes only in terms of the new types of employment which have become available to women, and have concentrated their attention on the possible correlation between the employment of women and female crime. In doing so, they have overlooked that woman's emancipation may express itself also in status increases in the family structure and in the handling of matters formerly reserved to the father as household head. Certainly there is a difference between the social situation and the temptation to commit unlawful behavior of a young girl who holds a white-collar or a factory job and lives at home with her parents, and that of a working mother who is either married or divorced and may either share the responsibilities of the household head or have to carry them alone.

Over and beyond the neglect of this aspect of social emancipation, the authors who have paid attention only to the relationship between the employment of women and female crime seem to have assumed that the social advances of the female sex are reflected in an even upswing of employment opportunities for women over the years. The amount of unconcern about the actual employment situation of women in the years used for an analysis of the quantitative movement of female crime is amazing. Obviously, the ups and downs in the employment of women which are caused by business depressions, economic and family readjustments after war periods, and interferences by recent ideologies such as National Socialism[7] have also to be considered before meaningful interpretations of changes in the female crime rate over the course of time can be made. Furthermore, not all jobs offer equal opportunities for crime, and occupational analyses of offender samples have indicated that women who are engaged in factory work have a rather low criminal liability, as will be shown at a later stage of this study.

It is not surprising, therefore, that authors who have neglected such considerations have produced seemingly contradictory evidence regarding the correlation between the emancipation of women and female crime. The nature and the degree of such apparent contradictions can be gathered from Table 5.

In view then of the impossibility of overcoming the index difficulties in the study of female crime by international comparisons in this case, any attempt to give an answer to our question would have to be abandoned at the present stage of research, if the literature did not contain further material. Fortunately, however,

TABLE 5

APPARENT TREND INDICATIONS OF THE GENERAL FEMALE CRIME RATE IN
VARIOUS COUNTRIES*

Country	Type of Ratio	Test Period	Increase	Decrease
United States (Mass.) (a)	Ratio of arrests to female population over 14 years of age	1896 to 1907		From 0.988 to 0.894
Germany (b)	Convictions of women per 100,000 female adults	1882-91 to 1892-1901	From 375 to 394	
Germany (c)	Convictions of women per 100,000 female adults	1902 to 1912		From 390 to 377
Germany (d)	Convictions of women per 100,000 female adults	1930 to 1936		From 304 to 206
Austria (e)	Convictions of women per 100,000 female adults (Serious crimes only)	1869 to 1900		From 36 to 34.4
Belgium (f)	Accusations of women per 1,000 females in the general population	1865-67 to 1883-85	From 1.82 to 2.52	
Finland (g)	Convictions of women per 100,000 female adults	1906-28	From 146 to 402	
England (h)	Convictions of women per 100,000 female adults (Indictable offenses only)	1931-38	From 41 to 53	

* Based on (a) Mary Conyngton, "Relation between Occupation and Criminality of Women," in *Report on Conditions of Woman and Child Wage-Earners in the United States*, XV (1911), 61st Congress, 2nd Session, Senate Document No. 645, p. 60; (b) Aschaffenburg, *op. cit.*, p. 161; (c) Georg von Mayr, *Statistik und Gesellschaftslehre*, III (1917), p. 742; (d) Ernst Roesner, "Zur Frage der weiblichen Kriminalität," discussed in *Monatsschrift für Kriminalbiologie und Strafrechtsreform*, XXVIII (1937), Sprechsaal, p. 485; (e) Hugo Herz, "Die Kriminalität des Weibes nach den Ergebnissen der neueren österreichischen Statistik," *Archiv für Kriminal-Anthropologie*, XVIII (1905), 291; (f) Camille Jacquart, *La Criminalité Belge 1868-1909*, p. 72; (g) Hans Hermann Burchardt, *Kriminalität in Stadt und Land*, p. 92; (h) Home Office, *Criminal Statistics, England and Wales, 1938* (London, 1940), p. xxx.

it also includes studies of test situations in which the social emancipation of women took a spectacular development and which permit international comparisons which show a coincidence of trends. These investigations have utilized the accentuation of the equalization process between women and men in World War I and are supported by data showing the movement of the female crime rate in the Franco-Prussian War of 1870-71.

Data for a number of countries indicate a similar trend in World War II.

In World War I the social roles of women increased temporarily to such a degree that the traditional division of labor between the sexes was completely disrupted. Women whose husbands left for the armed services had to assume the role of the family head. Their dealings with the outside world had to cover a whole range of contacts normally handled by their husbands. They came in touch with governmental authorities as well as with business people in all the aspects of life which had been previously covered by the activities of their husbands. They had to take over the husbands' businesses and farms. Reduction or loss of income through the departure of fathers and husbands forced them into economic pursuits which had been unknown to them before. The manpower demands of the war economy, together with the depletion of the ranks of male personnel, opened for women many job opportunities which had not been available to them in the prewar period. Women entered factories and offices, as well as other lines of employment, in much greater numbers than ever before. They were hired as trolley-car conductors, railroad brakemen, letter carriers, and even as farm hands. Many of the lower government services accepted them for the first time. Most of these changes in the social roles of women would have come about anyway in the course of social evolution, but only slowly and gradually. Now they were brought into sudden, if sometimes only temporary, existence. Correspondingly, a sudden onrush of temptations and opportunities for crime confronted women in those years.[8] That similar conditions reoccurred during World War II is within everyone's memory. They characterize every war which is carried on by citizens' armies.

The influence of such conditions on the female crime rate can already be measured for the period of the Franco-Prussian War. In 1870 there were 18 women convicted by the French trial juries per every 100,000 women in the population. In 1871 the number rose to 27, in 1872 to 33, and it remained at the same level in 1873.[9] It is worth noting that these figures show a continued increase in the first postwar year and stability in the second. This time lag in decline after the end of the war appears also in other instances, as will be seen below.

For World War I the material covers several belligerent countries. The trend similarity for these various countries is so pronounced that one's reluctance to put any trust in the index value of general crime rates regarding the problem at hand begins to weaken.

The writer tried to collect and work up the most detailed material available in the literature from the point of view of comparability, with the following results.

TABLE 6

YEARLY CONVICTION RATES OF WOMEN OFFENDERS IN FRANCE, GERMANY, AND HUNGARY, DURING AND AFTER WORLD WAR I, PER 100,000 WOMEN IN THE RESPECTIVE POPULATIONS*

Year	Total Court Convictions in France	Total Court Convictions in Germany	Total Convictions for Major Offenses (Verbrechen and Vergehen[a]) in Hungary
1914	134	311	103
1915	169	296	164
1916	190	334	186
1917	194	392	227
1918	229	482	—
1919	233	340	— } b
1920	264	475	—
1921	255	515	239
1922	204	451	308
1923	167	528	379
1924	161	467	357
1925	175	377	282
1926	190	356	236

* Based on absolute incidence figures reproduced by Hacker, "Soziale Kapillarität und Kriminalität," pp. 356, 359; population figures in *Annuaire Statistique*, XLII (1926), 13; *Statesman's Yearbook*, 1917, p. 690; and Liepmann, *op. cit.*, p. 136.

[a] Germany, Austria, and Hungary have a threefold classification of offenses: *Verbrechen, Vergehen,* and *Übertretungen. Verbrechen* is the category for serious offenses, *Übertretungen* that for minor offenses, and *Vergehen* represent a middle group. *Verbrechen* correspond roughly to the American category of felonies, *Vergehen* to misdemeanors, and *Übertretungen* to petty or summary offenses.

[b] No figures were published for these years in Hungary.

Notwithstanding the somewhat erratic character of some of the figures contained in this table, the increase of the general female crime rate in the war years is unmistakable for all three countries. Furthermore, the figures show also the continuation of this trend of increase in the postwar years and a trend reversal with the mitigation of postwar conditions in each case. Thus, the data seem to corroborate the hypothesis of the correlation between the emancipation of women and the rise in the female crime rate. In the war years when male manpower became depleted and women assumed many roles formerly reserved to men, female crime rates rose. After the returning men resumed their positions in civilian life and the prewar division of labor between the sexes was restored, female crime rates fell.

Statistical material for World War II does not seem to be similarly worked up in the literature, but the sex distribution of arrests compiled from the fingerprint records of the Federal Bureau of Investigation permits the following analysis for the United States.

TABLE 7

DISTRIBUTION OF ARRESTS BY SEX IN THE UNITED STATES, 1940-47, AS REFLECTED IN FBI FINGERPRINT RECORDS*

Year	Total	Male	Female
1940	609,013	557,063	51,950
1941	630,568	572,769	57,799
1942	585,988	515,635	70,353
1943	490,764	411,642	79,122
1944	488,979	405,379	83,600
1945	543,852	459,708	84,144
1946	645,431	576,689	68,742
1947	734,041	658,650	75,391

* Based on *Uniform Crime Reports*, XI (1940), No. 4, p. 204; XII (1941), No. 4, p. 203; XIII (1942), No. 2, p. 86; XIV (1943), No. 2, p. 87; XV (1944), No. 2, p. 91; XVI (1945), No. 2, p. 113; XVII (1946), No. 2, p. 116; XVIII (1947), No. 2, p. 115. The figures include juvenile delinquency in large cities.

Although this table shows only absolute incidence figures, a rise of female criminality in the war years appears unmistakably from the data. At first, the compilers of the reports expressed some caution against ascribing the increase in the female arrest figures apparent in their fingerprint analyses to an increase in the actual volume of crime.[10] The increase of the female records became so pronounced, however, that it can be safely regarded as an indication of a real increase in the incidence of female crime. Actually, the compilers dropped their cautious warnings against such a conclusion in the reports for 1944 and 1945.[11] The decline of the male arrest figures was due to the fact that large numbers of men in the ages of highest criminal liability served in the armed forces and were thus removed from general social circulation.

A similar, though not identical, picture appears from British data regarding persons convicted of indictable offenses during the war years.

TABLE 8

PERSONS FOUND GUILTY OF INDICTABLE OFFENSES, BY SEX, ENGLAND
AND WALES, 1938-45*

Year	Male	Female
1938	68,679	9,784
1939	68,100	9,958
1940	76,641	13,257
1941	90,736	17,147
1942	88,817	18,660
1943	86,369	18,895
1944	88,980	17,918
1945	99,305	16,956

* Based on Home Office, *Criminal Statistics, England and Wales, 1939-1945* (London, 1947), Appendix II, pp. 16-17.

Although it appears that male criminality in England and Wales did not decline during the war years and in fact showed considerable increase, female criminality increased at a much higher rate. In the year 1945 when the incidence of male crime had reached its peak for the period covered and female crime had already declined, the former stood only 45 per cent higher than at 1938, while female criminality stood 73 per cent above the prewar year level.

The question could now be raised whether this rise in female criminality is not also due to other factors than the increase of female employment and the temporary taking over of the role of family head by women. Are there not at work more fundamental forces which are related to a general rise in criminality during social upheavals and affect men as well as women, a fact which is obscured in war periods because so many men serve in the armed forces?

In order to answer this question, we have to try other lines of investigation than those pursued in the presentation of Tables 7 and 8. One attempt to get at the bottom of this matter would be the investigation of the movement of female crime rates in neutral countries. In such countries, men may also be withdrawn from social circulation because of mobilization of the armed services, but the social upheaval existent in belligerent countries does not occur. Women are not under the psychological strain of daily anxiety for the lives of their husbands and sons. Communication with husbands serving in the army is not interrupted to any degree comparable with the situation in belligerent countries. Certain age groups of men subject to military service in case of war may not be called up at all. On the other hand, the industrial boom accompanying modern warfare in neutral countries promotes the social emancipation of women in terms of employment opportunities, and some shifts in family responsibilities from husbands to wives may occur.

It is now interesting to see that the volume of recorded female crime in neutral countries during World War I shows a trend of increase similar to those in the belligerent countries, although not quite so pronounced.

For Switzerland, E. Hacker has worked up the material regarding the criminality in the Canton of Zurich and reported data which furnish the following interesting trend indication.

TABLE 9

TOTAL CONVICTIONS OF WOMEN PER 100,000 FEMALE POPULATION, CANTON OF ZURICH, 1914-20*

Year	Rate
1914	286
1915	263
1916	249
1917	270
1918	316
1919	235
1920	249

* Based on Hacker, *Die Kriminalität des Kantons Zürich*, p. 241.

It is immediately apparent that in neutral Switzerland the rise of the female crime rate seems to have started much later and subsided much earlier than in the belligerent countries. These variations, however, seem rather to corroborate than to contradict the hypothesis of the correlation between the emancipation of women and the rise in the female crime rate. It has to be considered that depletion of male manpower in neutral countries is less excessive and occurs more slowly than in belligerent countries. Female manpower, therefore, has to be tapped only at a later stage of the industrial boom accompanying modern warfare in neutral countries also. Furthermore, the reorganization of society and particularly of employment starts earlier than in countries which are affected by the problems of prisoners of war to be returned and combat soldiers to be readjusted after discharge.

For the Netherlands the monograph on female crime by Johanna C. Hudig gives certain absolute incidence figures for prewar, war, and postwar periods.

TABLE 10

YEARLY AVERAGES OF CONVICTIONS OF WOMEN OFFENDERS IN THE
ARRONDISSEMENT UTRECHT FOR SELECTED TIME PERIODS*

Year Groups	Yearly Averages of Female Convictions
1910-14	57
1915-18	85
1919-20	108

* Based on Hudig, *op. cit.*, p. 10.

It is regrettable that the combination in year groups does not permit tracing the development of the incidence of female crime for single years. This lack of data for single years may obscure the relationship between the incidence in the individual war years and the postwar years which we have been able to establish from the Swiss figures. It also would have been preferable, perhaps, to have conviction rates rather than absolute incidence figures. Even so, however, the rise of female crime in neutral Holland during World War I appears convincingly from these figures.

For World War II, published conviction data regarding crimes in neutral Sweden and nonbelligerent Denmark indicate also a pronounced rise in the volume of female crime.

TABLE 11

CONVICTIONS OF MEN AND WOMEN FOR SERIOUS OFFENSES,[a]
SWEDEN, 1937-42*

Year	Men	Index	Women	Index
1937	5,559	100	498	100
1938	5,985	108	533	107
1939	6,847	123	510	102
1940	6,779	122	658	132
1941	8,510	154	1,114	224
1942	10,986	198	1,559	313

[a] Serious offenses are offenses for which persons have been entered in the Penal Register of Sweden. As of January 1, 1943, there came into force a revision in the Swedish Penal Code and a delimitation of the group of offenses subject to registration in the Swedish Penal Register. This change excluded from registration an unknown number of offenses. Quantitative comparison of the data before and after January 1, 1943, is therefore impossible.

* Based on: *Sveriges officiella Statistik Röttsväsen, Brottsligheten*. Av. Statistika Centralbyrån, 1937-42. Table 8, pp. 76-77 (1937); Table 8, pp. 76-77 (1938); Table 4, pp. 22-23 (1939); Table 7, pp. 72-73 (1940); Table 4, pp. 22-23 (1941); Table 4, pp. 22-23 (1942).

TABLE 12

CONVICTIONS OF MEN AND WOMEN FOR OFFENSES AGAINST THE
PENAL CODE, DENMARK, 1937-43*

Year	Men	Index	Women	Index
1937	5,614	100	520	100
1938	5,426	97	576	111
1939	5,366	96	548	105
1940	5,646	101	654	126
1941	7,986	142	1,069	206
1942	10,767	192	1,698	326
1943	12,011	214	2,097	403

* Based on: *Danmarks Statistik, Statistike Meddelelser Kriminal Statistik*, København, 1933-43. Table VI, pp. 116-17 (1933-37); Table VI, pp. 52-53 (1938-39); Table VI, pp. 78-79 (1938-39); Table VI, pp. 50-51 (1940); Table VI, pp. 48-49 (1941); Table VI, pp. 50-51 (1942); Table VII, pp. 52-53 (1943).

The essential showing of these tables is, of course, the greater increase of female crime as compared with male crime. While the incidence of male convictions in both countries seems to have gone up about 100 per cent, the volume of female convictions in Sweden rose by about 200 per cent and in Denmark by about 300 per cent. Although the tables contain only absolute incidence figures, the population increase in these Scandinavian countries over the period of World War II was so small that the changes in crime volume clearly indicate a trend which cannot have been caused by population increases.

The question could still be raised whether the relatively greater increase of female crime was not due to the limited withdrawal of men from general social circulation because of military mobilization in Sweden and enforced labor service in Denmark. However, this does not seem to have been the case. Available statistics and population estimates for specific age groups in Denmark permit, for instance, a comparison between the increase in female and male crime in age brackets from which men were not drawn into forced labor. The crime rates for men and women in the age group 40 to 49 show that the criminality of men rose to a distinctly lesser degree than the criminality of women.

TABLE 13

CONVICTION RATES OF MEN AND WOMEN 40 TO 49 YEARS OF AGE FOR SERIOUS OFFENSES AGAINST THE PENAL CODE, DENMARK, 1937-38 AND 1943, PER 100,000 POPULATION*

Year	Men	Index	Women	Index
1937-38	272	100	22	100
1943	601	221	68	309

* Based on: *Danmarks Statistik, Statistike Meddelelser Kriminal Statistik,* København. Table VI, pp. 118-19 (1933-37); Table VI, pp. 54-55 (1938-39); Table VII, pp. 54-55 (1943); *Statistical Year Book of the League of Nations,* 1945, Table 3, p. 29.

It appears from this table that in an age group unaffected by the drainage of male manpower by enforced labor, male convictions about doubled and female convictions trebled in this period.

Another way of testing the question whether the rise of female crime during the periods of the last two world wars was really due to increase in the social emancipation of women and particularly in their employment opportunities would be concerned with the types of crimes committed. If the correlation between the phenomenon of social emancipation and the increase in female crime is to be meaningful, we should expect to find this increase primarily due to a growing incidence in crimes against property. Actually, this expectation appears corroborated by the German, Austrian, and Dutch experience during World War I. An analysis of the German material led Moritz Liepmann to produce the following table.

TABLE 14

ABSOLUTE FIGURES OF FEMALE CONVICTIONS, BY MAJOR OFFENSE
GROUPS, GERMANY, 1911-17*

Year	Total	Crimes against Government and Public Order	Crimes in Public Office	Crimes against the Person	Crimes against Property
1911	89,192	14,665	47	32,383	42,097
1912	91,653	15,228	36	34,004	42,385
1913	88,462	15,494	50	32,555	40,363
1914	77,870	13,469	45	27,617	36,739
1915	75,400	9,174	67	23,861	42,300
1916	86,400	7,908	162	25,214	53,116
1917	102,806	6,794	409	22,629	72,974

* Liepmann, *op. cit.,* p. 139.

This is perhaps the most revealing table contained in the
literature regarding the influence of social change on female
crime. The incidence of female convictions for crimes against
the person went down. The fact that women direct such criminal
attacks particularly against husbands and lovers[12] and that great
numbers of such persons were removed from the life sphere of
women during those years probably furnishes an explanation of
this phenomenon. On the other hand, crimes against property
led to 30,877 more convictions of women in 1917 than in 1911
while the increase in the total female criminality resulted only
in an increase of 13,614 convictions as between those years. The
rise in the incidence of female crimes against property was therefore disproportionately great. Now it could be said that the
economic distress and the threat of semistarvation prevailing in
the later war years may have caused this increase, and such an
opinion has actually been advanced.[13] It must not be overlooked,
however, that the rising tendency of female crimes against property is fairly evenly expressed from the first war year on and has,
therefore, come into existence before the catastrophic consequences of the war were felt. Thus, the new social roles and
opportunities opened up by the sudden emancipation of women
during the war seem to have been a factor.

The data for the war period in Austria present a similar picture. They were reported by Franz Exner for individual offense
types and do not permit working up to full comparability with
Liepmann's presentation. According to him, the number of fe-

male convictions for serious crimes against the person was, for instance, in 1913 (no figures were published for 1914) 57, but only 45 in 1916, and only 32 in 1918. On the other hand, there were 831 female convictions for serious crimes against property in 1913, 1,722 such convictions in 1916, and even 3,985 in 1918. Although these figures are not crime rates but only absolute conviction figures and refer only to the crime category of *Verbrechen*, the similarity in the relative decrease of attacks against the person and the tremendous increase in crimes against property can be gathered from them beyond any reasonable doubt.

Exner concluded his analysis of these data with the statement that the criminality of women in Austria became during the war years simply criminality against property, and explained this partly by an increase in opportunities and partly by an increase in needs.[14] In making this statement, he did not take into consideration how largely the criminality of women is actually masked, but the basis of his statement, namely, the great increase of female crimes against property in that period, can hardly be contested.

The Hudig material for the Netherlands is even more significant in this respect. In that country the factor of economic distress did not come into play, and still the rise in female crime during World War I was almost entirely due to crimes against property. This becomes immediately apparent from the following table.

TABLE 15

YEARLY AVERAGES OF FEMALE CONVICTIONS, BY MAJOR OFFENSE GROUPS, IN THE ARRONDISSEMENT UTRECHT FOR SELECTED TIME PERIODS[*]

Year Group	Crimes against the Person	Crimes against Property	Sex Offenses[a]
1910-14	30	27	—
1915-18	23	59	2
1919-20	28	78	3

[*] Hudig, *op. cit.*, p. 10.

[a] In Continental countries, prostitution is not forbidden by law but only regulated by the police.

The American data for the period of World War II support but do not exactly parallel these European data. The fingerprint records of the Federal Bureau of Investigation suggest that arrests for female crimes went up in all offense groups, but particularly so in the categories of sex offenses and petty crime.

TABLE 16

FEMALE ARRESTS FOR VARIOUS OFFENSE GROUPS IN THE UNITED STATES, 1940-47, AS REFLECTED IN FBI FINGERPRINT RECORDS*

Year	Arrests for Crimes against the Persona	Arrests for Crimes against Propertyb	Arrests for Sex Crimes and Petty Offensesc
1940	3,929	8,434	23,819
1941	4,387	8,417	28,555
1942	4,880	9,227	37,510
1943	4,675	10,041	43,384
1944	5,279	10,875	44,670
1945	5,844	12,164	45,808
1946	5,057	11,649	36,223
1947	6,199	13,083	39,564

* Based on same sources as Table 7.
a Figures refer to homicides and assaults.
b Figures refer to robbery, burglary, larceny, embezzlement and fraud, arson, forgery, and buying, receiving, etc., stolen property.
c Figures refer to prostitution and commercialized vice, other sex offenses, drunkenness, vagrancy, and disorderly conduct.

It is apparent from this table that the increase in the general crime rate suggested by the total figures was largely due to the increase in arrests for sex crimes and petty offenses. In the last full war year, 1944, property crimes appeared to have increased only 29 per cent over the 1940 figure and crimes against the person 35 per cent, while sex crimes and petty offenses seemed to have gone up 88 per cent. This apparent difference between the wartime experience with female criminality in the United States during World War II and that of Germany, Austria, and the Netherlands in World War I has of course to be understood primarily in terms of the differential reaction to violations of sex morality in this and continental countries. As pointed out above, prostitution on the continent is not forbidden by law but only regulated by the police. The whole increase in prostitution during World War I, therefore, did not affect the volume of female criminality in Germany, Austria, and the Netherlands. In England, World War II led apparently to a marked increase in property crimes but this increase was also more than paralleled by relatively stronger increases in other types of crimes.

TABLE 17

WOMEN FOUND GUILTY OF INDICTABLE OFFENSES, BY MAJOR OFFENSE GROUPS, ENGLAND AND WALES, 1938-45 *

	Violence against the Person	Property Crimes a	Sexual Offenses b
1938	228	9,042	92
1939	211	9,264	79
1940	200	12,648	69
1941	218	16,343	137
1942	259	17,492	222
1943	372	17,459	286
1944	392	16,649	238
1945	469	15,553	259

* Based on Home Office, *Criminal Statistics, England and Wales, 1939-1945* (London, 1947), Appendix I, pp. 14-15.

a Figures refer to larceny, breaking and entering, receiving, frauds, and false pretenses.

b Figures refer to sodomy, rape, incest, procuration, abduction, and bigamy.

These English data besides showing an increase in property crimes show an interesting increase in female crimes of violence against the person and of serious sex offenses. In order to understand this phenomenon it is necessary to remember that up to the invasion of Europe by the Allies the British army was largely concentrated in the home country and that the Island had also to accommodate very large numbers of American soldiers in preparation of the invasion. Furthermore, there were Polish, Free French, and Canadian soldiers stationed in that country. Considerable numbers of such soldiers passed through the Island also after the invasion. Thus, male-female relations with their potential of friction and criminal attack resulting therefrom were not reduced as they were in the continental countries analyzed for their criminality experience during World War I. They actually increased in numbers. Against this background the differential development of female criminality against the person in England during World War II and in Germany and Austria during World War I is understandable.

As to Sweden, the following table suggests considerable increases in female property crimes and even higher increases in female crimes of violence during World War II.

TABLE 18

WOMEN CONVICTED OF SERIOUS OFFENSES, BY MAJOR OFFENSE GROUPS,
SWEDEN, 1937-42*

Year	Crimes of Violence	Index	Offenses against Property	Index	Offenses against Public Order
1937	75	100	382	100	5
1938	72	96	433	113	5
1939	63	84	422	110	3
1940	112	149	525	137	6
1941	212	283	872	228	5
1942	277	369	1,233	323	14

* Based on the same sources as Table 11.

In Denmark the rise of property crimes and crimes of violence seems to have been about equally great.

TABLE 19

WOMEN CONVICTED OF SERIOUS OFFENSES AGAINST THE PENAL CODE, BY MAJOR
OFFENSE GROUPS, DENMARK, 1937-43*

Year	Crimes of Violence	Index	Offenses against Property	Index	Offenses against Morality
1937	66	100	391	100	40
1938	77	117	412	105	50
1939	63	96	401	103	39
1940	76	115	489	125	41
1941	119	180	849	217	14
1942	213	323	1,363	349	38
1943	278	421	1,673	428	24

* Based on the same sources as Table 12.

With regard to both countries we are again faced with the task of explaining the substantial increase of female crimes of violence which paralleled the increase of female crimes against property. Again we must consider that the drainage of men from social circulation and potential areas of friction with women which took place in Germany and Austria during World War I did not occur in these countries. Minor shifts due to mobilization and enforced labor in Sweden and Denmark respectively occurred but their quantitative impact was much less than the wartime impact in the central European countries. Denmark furthermore was under military occupation by Germany.

We come now to the conclusion of our analysis. The indications of similar trends in various countries and at various periods of time show that even the questionable indices used so far seem to have been sufficient for a corroboration of the hypothesis that an increase in female crimes against property is a concomitant of the social emancipation of women. If that is so, we have still to ask what the consequences of this phenomenon may be on the movement of woman's total criminality in the course of time. The problem to be considered is the influence of the social changes in woman's position in our society on the sum total of woman's roles. Has woman's assumption of occupational pursuits formerly reserved for men freed her from those other roles which were previously her only ones and which, as we have seen, so largely mask her criminality? An affirmative answer to this question could suggest that any possible increase in female criminality caused by the new opportunities for female crime in the economic sphere may well be outweighed by the loss of opportunities in the sphere of the home. This, however, does not seem to be the case. Woman with all her success in getting access to new fields and new social roles has not been able to get rid of her more traditional functions. She still is the homemaker, the rearer of children, and the shopper. Man—albeit grudgingly—has accepted her as a competitor, but he has as yet refused to become her substitute in the social sphere. Thus, with her burden of social functions increased, it seems probable that her opportunities for crime have not just changed but increased correspondingly. Only against the background of this sociological consideration is it possible to accept the suggestion of the material so far available that the total volume of female crime has increased as a result of the progressing emancipation of women in our society.

NOTES

1 Pike, *op. cit.*, p. 527; Colajanni, *op. cit.*, pp. 96-106; Loosjes, *op. cit.*, p. 61; Parmelee, *op. cit.*, p. 244; Bishop, *Women and Crime*, pp. 4-5; Kellor, *Experimental Sociology*, pp. 159-71; Herx, *op. cit.*, p. 28; Lombroso Ferrero, "I Delitti Femminili e le Nuove Professioni della Donna," *Archivio di Antropologia Criminale*, L (1930), 839-42.

2 Mary Conyngton, "Relation between Occupation and Criminality of Women," in *Report on Conditions of Woman and Child Wage-Earners in*

the United States, XV (1911), 61st Congress, 2nd Session, Senate Document No. 645; Aschaffenburg, *op. cit.*, p. 161; Hugo Herz, "Die Kriminalität des Weibes nach den Ergebnissen der neueren österreichischen Statistik," *Archiv für Kriminal-Anthropologie*, XVIII (1905), 292; Georg von Mayr, *Statistik und Gesellschaftslehre*, III (1917), 742-43.

8 Reckless, *Criminal Behavior*, pp. 97-98.

4 Sellin, *Research Memorandum on Crime in the Depression*, pp. 73-78; Reckless, *Criminal Behavior*, p. 98.

5 Dorothy S. Thomas, *Social Aspects of the Business Cycle*, p. 37.

6 Von Mayr, *op. cit.*, pp. 414, 418.

7 Franz Exner, "Die Reichskriminalstatistik 1935-1938," *Monatsschrift für Kriminalbiologie und Strafrechtsreform*, XXXIII (1942), 103.

8 Exner, *Krieg und Kriminalität in Österreich*, pp. 146-47; James H. S. Bossard, "War and the Family," *American Sociological Review*, VI (1941), 341-42.

9 Based on absolute incidence figures reproduced by E. Hacker, "Soziale Kapillarität und Kriminalität," *Monatsschrift für Kriminalbiologie und Strafrechtsreform*, XXVIII (1937), 354; and on population figures in *Annuaire Statistique*, XLII (1926), p. 13.

10 *Uniform Crime Reports*, XII, No. 2, p. 119; XIV, No. 1, p. 44.

11 *Uniform Crime Reports*, XV, No. 1, p. 48; XVI, No. 1, p. 63.

12 See Chapter II, pp. 13-14.

13 Sebastian von Koppenfels, *Die Kriminalität der Frau im Kriege*, pp. 43 ff.

14 Exner, *Krieg und Kriminalität in Österreich*, pp. 150, 155-56.

CHAPTER VII

THE SPECIFICITY OF FEMALE CRIME

As already indicated in the Introduction, the search for differences between the criminalities of either sex has been extended to various fields. Next to the question of a quantitative differential between the sum totals of male and female offenses, the problem of the sex specificity of female crime has attracted considerable attention. American authors particularly, but also a few Europeans, have investigated the differentials which may exist in the distribution of the offenses of men and women among the various types of crime. The material which they have produced seems to offer some valuable indications of the factors which influence the configuration of the criminality of women. An analysis of statistical data for the United States and Great Britain supplemented by Continental material referred to in the literature is therefore presented as a preliminary to the investigation of the causational aspects of female crime which will take up the final chapters of this study.

The problem in question has been formulated in various ways, but a common basis of approach can be discerned in all of them. Thus, the offense types in which the specificity of female crime has been said to express itself have been designated as "the more frequent offenses committed by women," as their "principal offenses," as their "prevailing crimes," as the crimes which "predominate" in their criminality, as "crimes which women generally engage in," as "conspicuous types" of female offenses, and reference has been made to crimes which occur with "striking frequency" among women.[1] These various expressions indicate that the research approach selected by the authors is of a quantitative nature. An analysis of the material presented now shows that the authors who have used these terms have actually been interested in two types of crime, namely, those in which women seem to participate more frequently than in others and those in which they show a relatively higher degree of participation than do men. Regarding the latter, the investigators have considered it as immaterial whether the crime in question was of great or small importance from the point of view of its incidence as such. Upon closer analysis, it seems that only the latter group is of significance for a study of sex specificity in crime because it is obvious that crimes in which women engage very frequently are meaningless for this question if men engage in these offenses with relatively equal frequency. Reckless has clarified this question by proposing that only crimes which show a strong deviation from the participation pattern of the other sex should be considered as sex specific.[2]

Since the problem has thus been conceived as one of a purely quantitative character, statistical difficulties have again to be considered. The dearth of other data has forced all investigators of this question to rely on official criminal statistics. The index difficulties in any such measurement of female crime have already been discussed at such length that to do so again seems unnecessary. It may be sufficient here to say that again any attempt to present an even tentative conclusion would have to be abandoned, if the various sets of data which have been produced in the literature were contradictory. Fortunately, however, this is not the case. Samples from various countries reveal upon consideration of known legal and cultural differences such a coincidence of indications regarding the problem at hand that it seems justified to accept their showing.

The sources which have been used in these various investigations cover the whole range from the sex composition of prison populations over the sex breakdowns of commitments to penal institutions and of conviction figures to the fingerprint record analyses, by sex, of the Federal Bureau of Investigation. In spite of their differences in the distance from the offense, these sources show about the same relationship for female and male participation in certain types of crime, as will be seen below.

Among the research techniques employed, four types can be distinguished: (1) comparisons among the numbers of women offenders per 100 men offenders for the various types of crime, (2) comparisons among the distributions of male and female cases within each 100 cases of the various offense types, (3) comparisons of the proportionate concentrations of the two sexes by offense type based on percentage breakdowns of the total criminality of either sex for the respective crime categories, and (4) comparisons of the general sex differential apparent in criminal statistics with the specific sex differentials for the various types of crime.

For purposes of clarity, the analysis here presented follows the classification of crimes according to the interest which they violate.

Crimes against the Person.

For the United States, commitment as well as arrest data show the criminal liability of women for homicides in normal times to be relatively higher than that of men. In 1940, for instance, the commitments of female offenders to federal and state institutions for murder and manslaughter represented 11.9 per cent of all commitments of female offenders to these institutions. The commitments of male offenders for these two crimes, however, represented only 4.9 per cent of all commitments of male offenders to these institutions in the same year. Similar differentials indicating a relative preponderance of women offenders among prisoners received for homicide appear year after year in the census statistics.[3] Part of these comparatively large divergencies may be due to the reluctance of our courts to pronounce a death sentence against a woman. That this, however, is not the full explanation appears from the fact that arrest data show also a relative preponderance of women with regard to homicide charges, at least in peacetime. In 1935, for instance, women arrested for homicide, as reflected in the fingerprint records received by the Federal Bureau of Investigation, represented 2.5 per cent of all female arrests, while men arrested on that charge amounted only to 1.7 per cent of all male arrests. In 1940 the corresponding proportionate concentration of female arrests for criminal homicide was 1.3 per cent and that of male arrests for the same offense category only 1 per cent.[4]

It is now interesting to see that this apparent relationship between male and female homicides changed in the war years. In
1942 the proportionate concentrations of arrests, as reflected in
the fingerprint analysis of the Federal Bureau of Investigation,
were still 1.1 per cent for female and only 1 per cent for male
offenders; in 1943, however, the relationship was already reversed,
being .8 per cent for female and 1 per cent for male offenders.
The trend continued in 1944, resulting in .7 per cent female and
1 per cent male offenders. The decline of female homicides suggested by these changes in the proportionate concentrations of
male and female cases is corroborated by the showing of the
absolute incidence figures. The female cases numbered 767 in
1942 and 627 in 1944.[5]

In the first full postwar year, 1946, however, we can already
notice a reversal of the war trend. The fingerprint records of the
FBI show equal proportionate concentrations of male and female
arrests for homicide. In 1947 the general prewar relationship of
female preponderance in homicide is reëstablished. One per cent
of the female arrests was based on homicide charges while only
.9 per cent of the male arrests were based on that charge.[6]

A possible explanation of this change has already been indicated in the preceding chapter. Many of the husbands went away,
and their being out of reach seems to have lowered the incidence
of women offenders in this type of crime.[7]

British indictment data corroborate the impression of a relative preponderance of female homicides. In the year 1930 the
women brought to trial in Assizes and Quarter Sessions for murder, attempt to murder, threats or conspiracy to murder, manslaughter, infanticide, and child destruction represented 6.3 per
cent of all women brought to trial in these courts. The male
trials for the same offenses represented only 2.3 per cent of all
male trials. In 1935 the corresponding percentages were 9.1 per
cent (female) and 2.4 per cent (male).[8] An analysis of the wartime
development of female participation in specific types of crime in
England cannot be presented because sufficiently detailed statistics are not available for the period after 1938.

As to European material, an Austrian investigation drew attention to the comparative frequency of homicides among female

THE SPECIFICITY OF FEMALE CRIME   81

offenders for a year half a century ago. According to that study, the Austrian statistics for the year 1899 revealed that while the general participation of women in the crime total was reflected by only 13.9 women in every 100 convictions, their participation in murder was reflected by 30.3 women in each 100 convictions for that particular crime.[9]

The German figures produced in the literature are not so pronounced and have a somewhat contradictory character. In 1896 the participation of women in crimes in general brought 17.9 female convictions for each 100 male convictions; in homicide, however, 22 women for each 100 men were convicted.[10] The Aschaffenburg material for 1909 is not worked up to the same degree but permits a computation of the corresponding figures with the result of a general female participation of 20 women per 100 men and a female participation in homicides of only 16.6 women per 100 men convicted.[11]

At first sight, homicide figures for Italy seem to be also contradictory to those presented for the Anglo-Saxon countries so far. For the three years 1885-89 they show only 3.4 women per 100 men convicted for this offense, while amazingly enough the general sex ratio in Italian convictions for these years was 50 women per 100 men. However, the Italian statistics list poisoning as a special offense while the United States and British data as well as those from Austria and Germany do not. Now the figures for poisoning reveal a specific sex ratio of 122.7 female per 100 male offenders convicted, and when poisonings and other forms of homicide are considered together, the specific sex ratio for all types of criminal killings except infanticides jumps up to 63 women per 100 men convicted. Addition of the infanticide figures which would be necessary to make the data really comparable with the American and British material is not possible because the investigation from which these figures are taken lists infanticides together with abortions. However, there can be no doubt that, if this procedure would be possible, the specific sex ratio shown above would appear still more unfavorable to women.[12]

We must again consider the comparability of the data. The United States and British figures presented here comprise all types of criminal homicide, regardless of victim and method. The

Austrian and German figures do not distinguish as to method but omit infanticide, which in the respective legal systems is a special offense which can only be committed by women. The Italian figures distinguish method as well as victim, show separate data for poisonings, and refer to a special crime, infanticide, but do not permit its inclusion in a total homicide figure as explained above.

Consideration of these facts suggests the following conclusions. The available American and British data as well as the various sex ratios referred to in the literature indicate that homicide is neither a typically male nor a typically female crime. Attacks upon human life are made by the members of either sex to such a degree that a specific deviation pattern between the male and female criminality in this respect cannot be found. The data have suggested, however, that if all types of victims and all methods of killings are included, the relative liability of women for homicide is greater than that of men. We have found indications of specificity only with regard to the victims particularly threatened by women offenders and the method of killing resorted to. The legal custom in European countries to establish infanticide as a special crime which refers in its definition only to woman as its perpetrator indicates a recognition by legislators of the frequency with which women, at least in countries where birth control is not widely practiced, direct their homicidal attacks upon the newborn. When this crime is committed by males it is classified as murder. The development of the American figures in wartime has suggested the amount of danger which women killers mean for their husbands. Finally, the Italian figures have corroborated the prevailing opinion that women resort to poison more often than to any other homicidal weapon.

Comparable material regarding assault can be presented only for the United States and England because the legal systems of the Continent, particularly those of Austria and Germany, cover the criminal behavior represented thereby in three different offense categories which in their sum total, however, would include more acts than those covered by the American and British data.

For the United States, prewar commitment figures now show

the following picture. In 1938 and 1940 the commitments to federal and state prisons and reformatories of male offenders for aggravated assaults represented approximately 5 per cent of all male commitments to these institutions while the corresponding female percentage was in round figures 7 per cent in both years. In 1939 the differential participation of women in commitments for this offense was even more pronounced: 5.1 per cent of all male offenders and fully 8.6 per cent of all female offenders so committed were convicted of aggravated assaults.[13]

Arrest data for the prewar years seem to corroborate this showing. In 1940, female arrests for assaults represented 6.3 per cent of all female arrests as reflected in the fingerprint records of the Federal Bureau of Investigation, while the respective male arrest figures were 5.5 per cent. In 1941, the female arrest percentage for assault was 6.4 per cent and the male arrest percentage for the same offense 6 per cent.[14]

Thus, the immediate prewar figures seemed to justify J. Edgar Hoover's statement that an average of 1,000 female criminals committed among others also more assaults than an average group of 1,000 male criminals.[15]

The arrest data for the war years, however, indicate also a change in the relationship between the female and the male proportionate concentration in assaults. From 1942 through 1944, the arrests of men for assaults represented in every year a higher percentage of all male arrests than the arrests of women did with regard to their arrest totals. In these years the male percentages were 6.6, 7.4, and 8 versus the female percentages of 5.9, 5.1, and 5.6 respectively. They thus show a yearly male average of 7.3 per cent of all male arrests against a yearly female average of 5.5 per cent of all female arrests.

For this offense, the postwar years up to the time of this writing have not brought a reëstablishment of the prewar relationship, although the figures for 1947, namely, a male arrest concentration of 8 per cent versus a female arrest concentration of 7.2 per cent, indicate that their relationship of the war years may be about to be reversed.[16]

In the case of the assaults by women, the absolute incidence figures did not go down as in the case of homicide. They actually rose from 4,113 in 1942 to 4,652 in 1944 and to 5,459 in 1947. It must be concluded, therefore, that here the change in the relationship between the female and the male proportionate concentrations was probably due to a greater rise of female crime in other offense categories which was not paralleled by a similar rise in male crime. In other words, the great increase in female sex offenses and petty crime kept the assault proportion down rather than a decrease in victims resulting in an actual decrease in incidence.

For England the official criminal statistics of the prewar years again corroborate the picture gained from the American data. There, women accused of "felonious" and "malicious wounding" represented 3.7 per cent of all women brought for trial in Assizes and Quarter Sessions in 1930, while for the same year male offenders brought for trial on that accusation represented only 3.2 per cent of all male offenders tried in these courts. The respective figures for 1935 are 4.3 per cent of the women offenders and 3.3 per cent of the male offenders tried.[17] Thus we have also in England a prewar picture of relative female preponderance for this offense type.

There is one crime against the person, however, which shows an unquestionable preponderance of women offenders, the abandonment of children. The social conditions governing the mother-child relationship in cases of illegitimacy account so clearly for this phenomenon that little statistical corroboration seems required. Suffice it to give the following figures. In 1896 there were 800 women convicted for this offense per 100 men so convicted in Germany, and in Austria in 1899 there were 93.8 convictions of women in every 100 cases. The Italian figures for this offense are reported together with the figures for abuse of the right of physical discipline. It may be of interest, however, that, in the years 1929 and 1930, out of every 100 convictions for this combined offense category 22 concerned women offenders, while for all crimes in 1929 only 19 and in 1930 only 16 out of every 100 persons convicted in Italy were women.[18]

It seems that only infanticides and the abandonment of children are clearly established as specifically female crimes as far as offenses against the person are concerned. However, infanticide is only a form of homicide and abandonment of children is only a form of offense against the family. We must, therefore, come to the conclusion that female sex specificity in crimes against the person cannot be found in the offense type so much as in the types of victims against whom the offense is directed and in the methods pursued by the offender.

Crimes against Property.

For this group of crimes the observation has been repeatedly made that larcenies are comparatively frequent among the crimes of women while predatory crimes with violence are definitely scarce.[19]

For the United States, the FBI data for 1940-47 indicate that larcenies show about the same proportionate concentrations in the criminality of the female as in that of the male sex, no matter whether it is peace or war. They produced, for instance, 10.2 per cent of the male and 10.3 per cent of the female arrests in 1940, 9.4 per cent of the male and 8.9 per cent of the female arrests in 1944, and 8.5 per cent of the male and 10.6 per cent of the female arrests in 1947.[20]

The German figures produced by Aschaffenburg for 1909 showed that 31.4 women were convicted of petit larceny per 100 men so convicted, while the relationship of all female to all male convictions was only 20 women per 100 men. Grand larceny, however, brought only 7.3 female convictions per 100 male convictions.[21] In 1936, the German sex differential for all convictions was 6.5 male for 1 female case, the differential for larceny (simple stealing), however, only 4 male for 1 female case.[22]

The Austrian figures for 1899 also show a sex differential unfavorable to women, the general differential for serious crimes (*Verbrechen*) being only 13.9 women to 86.1 men out of every 100 convictions, while the grand larceny differential was 19.5 women to 80.4 men in every 100 convictions for that offense.[23]

For England and Wales, the numbers of persons against whom the police proceeded for indictable offenses in 1930 show a general sex differential of 7 male for 1 female case, and for offenses against property without violence (usually theft), one of 6.3 male for 1 female case. The corresponding differentials in 1935 were substantially the same.[24]

Property crimes with violence on the other hand present a completely different picture.

The United States arrest figures analyzed by the Federal Bureau of Investigation are as follows:

TABLE 20

PROPORTIONATE CONCENTRATIONS OF ARRESTS FOR ROBBERY AND BURGLARY IN THE TOTAL ARREST GROUPS OF BOTH SEXES, AS REFLECTED IN FBI FINGERPRINT RECORDS, 1940-47*

Year	Robbery		Burglary	
	Male	Female	Male	Female
1940	2.3%	1.1%	6.1%	1.1%
1941	2.0	1.1	5.1	1.2
1942	2.2	0.8	4.7	0.8
1943	2.5	0.7	5.6	0.9
1944	2.6	0.7	6.0	1.0
1945	3.0	1.0	6.2	1.1
1946	3.1	1.3	5.9	1.3
1947	3.1	1.3	5.6	1.4

* Based on the same sources as Table 7.

The German material for 1896 shows the sex differential for robbery as even more accentuated than in the more recent American figures. It was 2.9 women for each 100 men convicted of this offense while the general sex differential for that year was 17.9 women per 100 men convicted.[25]

The Herz material gives the robbery differential with 4.8 women out of every 100 convictions, and it will be remembered that the general ratio in that set of data was 13.9 women out of every 100 convictions.[26]

Buying, receiving, etc., of stolen property presents a somewhat similar picture to that offered by larceny, although the position of the offense in the criminality of both sexes cannot be called exactly equal. With regard to the situation in the United States, the picture is the following. In the prewar year 1940 the FBI arrest analysis indicated .6 per cent of all male arrests and .5 per cent of all female arrests to have occurred on the basis of this charge. In 1941 and 1943 the respective male and female percentage figures were .5 per cent and .4 per cent. In the war years 1942 and 1944, however, the male arrests for this type of offense again constituted .6 per cent of all male arrests but the female arrests only .3 per cent of the female arrest totals.[27] The arrest data for 1946 and 1947 show complete equality in proportionate concentration for both sexes (.5 per cent for 1946, and .4 per cent for 1947). Thus, before the war both sexes showed almost equal relative criminal liability in this offense category, and in the war years the female liability dropped but was restored again after the war. Analysis of the absolute incidence figures underlying these percentages suggests that it was less the increase of female sex offenses and petty offenses than specific wartime conditions surrounding this offense which were the reasons of this apparent relative decline. The absolute incidence figures did not actually fall but they rose much less than, for instance, the female incidence of larceny. They did not follow the general trend of incidence of this representative crime against property. There must, therefore, have been special reasons for this lag. Now the thieves from whom women usually receive stolen goods are probably in the majority husbands, lovers, and sons. In other words, women act not so much as professional fences as in the role of family receivers. The wartime absence of family members who stole in the prewar years and the general economic conditions during the war which provided employment for men with previous criminal records seem to have relieved many a woman from this unenviable role.

The German figures suggest an even stronger participation of women in this type of offense than the American data. In 1896 there were 158.3 women convicted of this offense per 100 men in cases of repeated recidivism and 53.9 women per 100 men in cases of simple recidivism.[28] For 1909, the Aschaffenburg material, which does not consider cases of recidivism separately, shows 46.9 women convicted of this offense for every 100 men convicted thereof.[29]

For Italy, Lombroso draws attention to the fact that while on the average 6 women were condemned at the Assizes for each 100 men in the years 1885-89, the number of women convicted for receiving stolen goods was on the average 20.2.[30]

For arson, the United States arrest data suggest equal criminal liability for men and women. In 1940 the arrests of persons in both sex groups for this offense represented .2 per cent of the respective total arrest figures in each group, and through the years 1941-45 as well as the postwar years 1946 and 1947 the percentages were always .1 for both sexes.[31]

The English figures of trials for arson in Assizes and Quarter Sessions show .6 per cent of the male and 1.2 per cent of the female cases in 1930 and .8 per cent of the male and .5 per cent of the female cases in 1935 based on that offense.[32]

The German data for 1896 give the number of convictions of women for this crime with 21.8 per 100 men convicted as against a general sex ratio of 17.9 women per 100 men convicted.[33]

The Herz material for Austria shows that in 1899 the sex distribution for arson was 14.7 women and 85.2 men out of every 100 convictions, while the general distribution was 13.9 women and 86.1 men.[34]

In Italy, the conviction averages for 1885-89 produced 8.6 sentences against women for this crime per 100 convictions of men against the general average of 6 female per 100 male convictions at the Assizes.[35]

Thus, again no deviation in the distribution pattern sufficiently clear-cut and pronounced to justify a statement regarding sex specificity for arson can be found in the material.

In summary, the data regarding crimes against property lead to conclusions somewhat similar to those arrived at with respect to crimes against the person. Larceny, receiving stolen goods, and arson show relative criminal liabilities which are so close for men and women that no statement regarding any sex specificity can be made. Only crimes against property with violence seem to be characterized by a specifically higher liability of men. However, consideration of the female modus operandi in these offenses would rather suggest that in this offense group women confine themselves more to auxiliary roles than in others and therefore remain undetected to an even higher degree than usual. The wartime development of the arrest rate for buying, receiving, etc., of stolen goods has finally suggested a certain specificity in the types of thieves from whom women receive such goods. All this suggests again that the specificity of female crime has to be looked for rather in method and procedure than in the interests violated by certain offense categories.

Crimes against Sex Morality.

At first sight the participation of women in this group of crimes seems to be very different in the United States from that in Continental Europe. This apparent disparity is well illustrated in the two following statements. Barnes and Teeters say in their book *New Horizons in Criminology* that "we think of sex crimes —prostitution primarily—when we think of delinquency among girls and women," and all American authors who have discussed this question seem to share this opinion.[36] On the other hand, an authority like Franz Exner made the statement that "generally crimes against the morals are infrequent among women,"[37] and also the other European authors seem to mention only one offense against sex morality, procuring, as a crime which women commit more frequently than do men.[38]

This divergence of opinion is well reflected in the picture furnished by criminal statistics. The American arrest figures analyzed by the FBI show, for instance, the following ratios.

TABLE 21

PROPORTIONATE CONCENTRATIONS OF ARRESTS FOR SEX OFFENSES EXCEPT RAPE IN THE TOTAL ARREST GROUPS OF BOTH SEXES, AS REFLECTED IN FBI FINGERPRINT RECORDS, 1940-47*

Year	Male	Female
1940	1.9%	15.2%
1941	2.1	14.9
1942	2.2	13.6
1943	2.6	13.6
1944	2.8	13.0
1945	2.7	14.8
1946	2.9	14.4
1947	2.8	12.2

* Based on the same sources as Table 7.

Actually, these figures would have to be supplemented to a considerable extent by the female arrests for disorderly conduct and vagrancy which are in many instances only euphemisms covering police actions against women who engage in sex offenses,[39] and which spectacularly swelled the arrest figures during the war years.

The data regarding the specificity of female crime produced

by the European authors, however, do not even include prostitution and commercialized vice.

The explanation of this disparity is furnished, not by differentials in behavior, but by differences in cultural evaluations and their reflection in the substantive law as well as in the policy of prosecution. Reckless has indicated this situation pointedly by stating that prostitution and commercialized vice are "a peculiar liability for arrest and detention of females in American society."[40] However, that such behavior is just as predominant, if not more so, among the women of Europe as in the United States needs hardly any elaboration. It may suffice to point out that Lombroso was of the opinion that if prostitution were included in the European criminal statistics, the whole quantitative differential between the criminality of men and that of women would disappear.[41]

That prostitution is a specifically feminine form of behavior cannot be seriously questioned. To be sure, male prostitutes exist in the sphere of homosexuality and they may well be more numerous than has been generally assumed.[42] The ratio of their number to the number of female prostitutes, however, cannot be greater than the quantitative relationship between normal and abnormal sex expression. What we see then is a greater tendency among women to use their own sex for illicit gainful purposes as compared with such behavior among men. In this quantitative sense the female specificity of this type of behavior must be accepted. Furthermore, as already pointed out, prostitution as a criminal offense cannot be committed by men because of its statutory definition.[43] Thus, where prostitution is prohibited by the criminal law, it represents a specifically female crime.

Crimes against Sobriety and Good Health.

Of the offense types which fall under this group, drunkenness and violation of the narcotic drug laws have been mentioned by the American investigators in connection with the sex specificity of female crime.[44]

With regard to drunkenness, a confusion has arisen between the comparative frequency of this offense among other offenses committed by women and the degree of the criminal liability of women for drunkenness as compared with that of men. Drunkenness, certainly, ranks high among the offenses for which women are arrested, but it ranks even higher among the offenses for which men are so proceeded against. This fact has been noted by Reckless in his comparison of sex differentials which indicate 19 male for 1 female arrest on the basis of this offense while the general sex differential was only 13.4 men for 1 woman arrested.[45]

Violations of narcotic drug laws, however, show some indications of a higher relative liability of women than of men. This appears already in commitment figures. In 1938, 7.5 per cent of the female commitments stood against only 3.3 per cent of the male commitments under this category (felony and misdemeanor commitments). In 1943, the respective commitment percentages were 7 per cent female and 2.8 per cent male (felony commitments only).[46]

The following arrest data will give the comparative material for both offenses in the immediate prewar and the war period.

TABLE 22

PROPORTIONATE CONCENTRATIONS OF ARRESTS FOR DRUNKENNESS AND VIOLATIONS OF THE NARCOTIC DRUG LAWS, AS REFLECTED IN FBI FINGERPRINT RECORDS, 1940-47*

Year	Drunkenness		Violations of Narcotic Drug Laws	
	Male	Female	Male	Female
1940	19.4%	14.5%	0.5%	3.8%
1941	23.3	15.8	0.3	1.6
1942	26.0	16.4	0.2	0.2
1943	24.1	14.8	0.3	0.2
1944	22.6	15.5	0.4	0.3
1945	24.0	17.5	0.4	0.3
1946	23.9	18.7	0.4	0.4
1947	24.1	20.8	0.5	0.4

* Based on the same sources as Table 7.

From these drunkenness figures, it appears clearly that in spite of its comparative frequency this is certainly not an offense which characterizes the criminality of women. The data for violations of the drug laws, on the other hand, show a decline of female incidence since 1941, which expressed itself also in absolute incidence figures. This phenomenon defies any explanation at the present stage of research. We must conclude, therefore, that also in the group of crimes against sobriety and good health no category of offenses has been found which could with sufficient scientific justification be called a specifically female crime.

We are at the end of our survey and can take stock. In summary, all investigations of the differential participation of the sexes in the various types of crime seem to lead to the conclusion that except for violations of the sex mores prevailing in the United States, there is hardly any offense which could be considered as specifically female, if this term is reserved for those offenses in which the relative criminal liability of women far outweighs that of men. In crimes against the person, women appear as killers to at least the same relative degree as do men and in assaults the normal trend seems to be in the same direction. Only the victims appear to differ, infants, children, husbands, and lovers being the preferred victims of the woman offender. In crimes against property, it is only the divergence in the application of force which distinguishes the criminality of the two sexes. However, consideration of the roles which women are said to perform as the accessories of robbers and burglars and of the resulting difficulties in their apprehension indicate that it is more the type than the fact of participation in these crimes which accounts for the apparent differential. In buying, receiving, etc., stolen goods, we have seen by implication that it is more the person with whom the female receivers coöperate than the frequency with which they commit this offense, which seems to express a sex differential with regard to this crime category. In the sphere of crimes against sobriety and good health, we have had occasion to see that drunkenness, although a high liability of women, is still a higher one of men and that the available data for violations of the drug laws do not yet permit us to regard them as a crime with a specifically higher criminal liability of women than of men. Only prostitution cannot be questioned as a typically female offense, if the situation only in the United States is considered.

It is thus not so much the interest which women violate, or the degree to which they do so, as the victim which they choose, the person with whom they coöperate, the opportunities of which they avail themselves, and the part which they play in the actual perpetration of certain offenses which seem to express the sex specificity of female crime.

NOTES

1 Wood and Waite, *op. cit.*, pp. 237-38; Parmelee, *op. cit.*, p. 232; Barnes and Teeters, *op. cit.*, p. 571; Aschaffenburg, *op. cit.*, p. 158.

2 Reckless, *Criminal Behavior*, p. 100.

3 U. S. Bureau of the Census, *Prisoners in State and Federal Prisons and Reformatories, 1941*, p. 18 (giving the data for the years 1937-41); *1942*, p. 38; *1943*, p. 42; *1944*, p. 43; *1945*, p. 42.

4 *Uniform Crime Reports*, VI (1935), No. 4, p. 27; XI (1940), No. 4, p. 204.

5 *Uniform Crime Reports*, XIII (1942), No. 2, p. 86; XIV (1943), No. 2, p. 87; XV (1944), No. 2, p. 91.

6 *Uniform Crime Reports*, XVII (1946), No. 2, p. 116; XVIII (1947), No. 2, p. 115.

7 See Chapter VI, p. 70.

8 Based on Home Office, *Criminal Statistics, England and Wales, 1930* (London, 1932), pp. 35, 39; *1935* (London, 1937), pp. 35, 39.

9 Herz, *op. cit.*, p. 286.

10 Parmelee, *op. cit.*, p. 234.

11 Based on Aschaffenburg, *op. cit.*, Table XXXI, p. 159.

12 Roncoroni, "Influenza del Sesso sulla Criminalità in Italia," *Archivio di Psichiatria, Science Penali ed Antropologia Criminale*, XIV (1893), 5-6.

13 U. S. Bureau of the Census, *Prisoners in State and Federal Prisons and Reformatories, 1938*, p. 13; *1939*, p. 9; *1940*, p. 7.

14 *Uniform Crime Reports*, XI (1940), No. 4, p. 204; XII (1941), No. 4, p. 203.

15 Barnes and Teeters, *op. cit.*, p. 571.

16 *Uniform Crime Reports*, XIII (1942), No. 2, p. 86; XIV (1943), No. 2, p. 87; XV (1944), No. 2, p. 91; XVIII (1947), No. 2, p. 115.

17 Based on Home Office, *Criminal Statistics, England and Wales, 1930* (London, 1932), pp. 35, 39; *1935* (London, 1937), pp. 35, 39.

18 Parmelee, *op. cit.*, pp. 234, 235; Niceforo, *op. cit.*, pp. 680, 682.

19 Aschaffenburg, *op. cit.*, p. 159; Herz, *op. cit.*, p. 287; Wood and Waite, *op. cit.*, p. 238; Barnes and Teeters, *op. cit.*, p. 571.

20 *Uniform Crime Reports*, XI (1940), No. 4, p. 204; XV (1944), No. 2, p. 91; XVIII (1947), No. 2, p. 115.

21 Aschaffenburg, *op. cit.*, p. 159.

22 Reckless, *Criminal Behavior*, p. 102.

23 Herz, *op. cit.*, p. 286.

24 Home Office, *Criminal Statistics, England and Wales, 1930* (London, 1932), pp. 93, 95; *1935* (London, 1937), pp. 92-93.

25 Parmelee, *op. cit.*, p. 234.

26 Herz, *op. cit.*, p. 287.

27 *Uniform Crime Reports*, XI (1940), No. 4, p. 204; XII (1941), No. 4, p. 203; XIII (1942), No. 2, p. 86; XIV (1943), No. 2, p. 87; XV (1944), No. 2, p. 91; XVII (1946), No. 2, p. 116; XVIII (1947), No. 2, p. 115.

28 Parmelee, *op. cit.*, p. 234.

29 Aschaffenburg, *op. cit.*, p. 159.

30 Lombroso, *op. cit.*, p. 184.

31 *Uniform Crime Reports,* XI (1940), No. 4, p. 204; XII (1941), No. 4, p. 203; XIII (1942), No. 2, p. 86; XIV (1943), No. 2, p. 87; XV (1944), No. 2, p. 91; XVI (1945), No. 2, p. 113; XVII (1946), No. 2, p. 116; XVIII (1947), No. 2, p. 115.

32 Based on Home Office, *Criminal Statistics, England and Wales, 1930* (London, 1932), pp. 37, 39; *1935* (London, 1937), pp. 37, 39.

33 Parmelee, *op. cit.,* p. 234.

34 Herz, *op. cit.,* pp. 286-87.

35 Lombroso, *op. cit.,* p. 184.

36 Barnes and Teeters, *op. cit.,* p. 571; Harry Best, *Crime and the Criminal Law in the United States,* p. 174; John Lewis Gillin, *Criminology and Penology,* 3rd ed., pp. 53-54.

37 Exner, *Krieg und Kriminalität in Österreich,* p. 157.

38 Exner, *ibid.;* Aschaffenburg, *op. cit.,* p. 158; Herz, *op. cit.,* p. 287; Melegari, *op. cit.,* p. 529; Pollitz, *op. cit.,* p. 28; Niceforo, *op. cit.,* p. 681.

39 Breckinridge and Abbott, *op. cit.,* p. 37.

40 Reckless, *Criminal Behavior,* p. 100.

41 Lombroso, *op. cit.,* pp. 185-86.

42 Alfred C. Kinsey, Wardell B. Pomeroy, Clyde E. Martin, *Sexual Behavior in the Human Male,* p. 596.

43 See Chapter V, p. 55.

44 Best, *op. cit.,* p. 176; Barnes and Teeters, *op. cit.,* p. 571; Wood and Waite, *op. cit.,* p. 237; Reckless, *Criminal Behavior,* pp. 100-101; Gillin, *op. cit.,* p. 53.

45 Reckless, *Criminal Behavior,* p. 100.

46 Based on U. S. Bureau of the Census, *Prisoners in State and Federal Prisons and Reformatories, 1938,* p. 9; *1943,* p. 42.

CHAPTER VIII

PERSONAL CHARACTERISTICS OF FEMALE OFFENDERS: AGE

The material in the literature regarding the personal characteristics of female offenders is of unequal value for an understanding of their criminality. Questions of age, marital status, occupation, intelligence, and race have been investigated to some extent, but the findings regarding the influence of the age and the conjugal factor upon female crime are much richer and seemingly more reliable than the findings regarding the others. In the following analysis the emphasis will, therefore, be placed on the age and marital status liabilities apparent among female offenders. The material regarding occupations, intelligence, and race will be presented more because of its value as a basis for further research than because of its contribution to our present stage of knowledge.

It must be kept in mind, however, that all these descriptive characteristics of offenders show only a distant relationship to questions of causation. They can only guide research into meaningful channels and direct it to promising spots, but they cannot give any answer sufficiently specific to justify its presentation as an aspect of causation itself.

Even with this reservation, a distinction must still be drawn between the age factor and the other personal characteristics of offenders. Because of its most common nature, it seems logical to discuss the age factor first and then to gradually narrow down the descriptive inquiry to the other personal characteristics of offenders. Accordingly, this chapter will deal only with the material on age and female crime as an introductory step to the analysis of the material regarding the other personal characteristics of women criminals. The latter will then be presented in the next chapter.

The Age Liabilities of Female Offenders.

The material in the literature regarding the differences between women and men offenders with regard to age indicates three basic observations. Some authors have found that girls seem to get started on delinquency later than do boys. Others have made investigations which led them to the conclusion that the age of highest incidence in crime comes later for women than it comes for men. A few, finally, have pointed out that a relatively greater part of female crime than of male crime is to be found in middle age and the more advanced age brackets.

Of necessity, the research into these sex differentials by age has to be statistical. The material so far available had to be drawn from official criminal statistics which we have come to consider as particularly unreliable where female-male incidence relationships of crime are concerned. The possibility of errors in studies which analyzed material from only one official source is, therefore, very great. It is even more so when sex ratios calculated on the basis of official criminal statistics are used. The method here pursued in combating this danger is again reliance on international statistical comparisons and, furthermore, preference for those research techniques which abstain from using sex ratios for index purposes.

In the following pages the dissimilarities between the age liabilities of the two sexes will first be presented on the basis of United States and English data. These data will be supplemented by Continental material in the form in which it was analyzed in the literature. For purposes of retesting and greater clarity, however, some of the data will then be subjected to a unified statistical treatment covering all aspects of interest in the relation between age and crime and keeping free from the use of sex ratios.

Following this program, we have now to turn to an analysis of the available material in the form in which it usually is presented.

The Later Start.

There is evidence from various countries which indicates that relatively more boys than girls get into early trouble with the courts. An age analysis of the juvenile court cases in the United States, for instance, showed that in 1934 delinquents under 14 years of age contributed 43 per cent of the boys' and only 29 per cent of the girls' cases.[1] Analysis of the 1930 data for England and Wales shows that 13.1 percent of the males convicted (or charge proved) and only 5.2 per cent of the females convicted (or charge proved) were under 14 years old. In 1935 the males under 14 years of age who were found so guilty represented 21.6 per cent of all male offenders convicted of indictable offenses, the females under 14, however, only 7.3 per cent of the total of women convicted of such offenses.[2] Data from Germany and Italy permit similar observations as will be seen from Table 27.

Later Peak Incidence.

Data regarding the later age at which women reach the highest incidence of their criminal activities are here presented for the United States, England, Belgium, Germany, and Italy.

Arrest data for New York State covering the period 1935-40 show that persistently during that six-year period the age of highest incidence for major offenses was reached later by women than by men.

TABLE 23

AGES OF HIGHEST INCIDENCE OF ARRESTS FOR MAJOR OFFENSES, ACCORDING TO SEX, NEW YORK STATE, 1935-40*

Year	Male	Female
1935	19	21-24
1936	19	21-24
1937	19	21-24
1938	19	25-29
1939	16-18	25-29
1940	19	25-29

* Based on the *Annual Reports of the Commissioner of Correction on Crime Statistics for 1935* (p. 206); *1936* (p. 198); *1937* (p. 332); *1938* (p. 458); *1939* (p. 380); and *1940* (p. 390).

The same phenomenon seems to exist when only felonies are considered. It has been observed that the male incidence of acts which fall under this category reaches its peak between the ages of 16 to 25 years, at which age period the incidence of felonies committed by women is at a low, and that the latter rises briskly between the ages of 26 and 30 years.[3]

The very detailed age breakdowns of the official British statistics for the prewar period show that the same relationship between the male and female ages of peak criminality exists also in England and Wales, although the ages of highest incidence for both sex groups seem to be reached somewhat earlier in those countries than in the United States.

The British statistics reported for the years up to 1938 crime rates of persons found guilty of indictable offenses for single years of age from 8 years to 20 years, for the two five-year periods of the twenties, for ten-year periods for the thirties, forties, and fifties, and then a lump rate for the sixty plus group. On that basis they showed, for instance, for the year 1938 the peak incidence of convictions for males to be 13 years and for females 19 years.[4]

Belgian figures giving crime rates by age and sex have been reported in the literature for several three-year periods between 1899 and 1908. In the periods 1899 to 1901, 1904 to 1906, and 1906 to 1908, the age group of highest incidence for male convictions was throughout 21 to 25 years, that for female convictions, however, 25 to 30 years in the first period, and 30 to 35 years in the two others.[5]

With regard to Italy, Dora Melegari drew attention to the fact that the criminality of women reached its culmination later than that of men,[6] and material presented by Alfredo Niceforo for the years 1929 and 1930 corroborated her general statement, showing the age of highest incidence for male convictions to be in the age group 25-30 and for women in the age group 30-40.[7]

German data which have been analyzed in the literature partly confirm and partly weaken the so far impressive evidence. According to Ernst Roesner, the highest male conviction rate in the ten-year period 1886 to 1895 fell into the age group 18 to 21, while the age group 30 to 39 showed the highest frequency of female convictions. In 1929, on the other hand, the Roesner material shows the age of highest conviction frequency for both sexes to have been in the age group 21 to 24.[8] The equality in the ages of highest incidence of men and women offenders suggested by the German figures for 1929, however, seems to have been considered exceptional, because seven years later Liselotte Herx reported again the general observation that women reached the peak incidence of their offenses later than men.[9]

Greater Criminal Liability of Women in the Higher Age Groups.

There seems to exist also statistical evidence which indicates a higher proportionate concentration of female crime than of male crime in the higher age groups.

In the state of New York, the arrests of women who gave their age as 35 years or more represented 35 per cent of all women arrested in 1940 while the arrests of men in the corresponding age groups represented only 29 per cent of all men arrested in that year. A breakdown by race, however, shows that this phenomenon is limited to the white group. Of the negro women arrested, only 22 per cent gave their age as 35 years or more while, of the negro men arrested, 25 per cent fell into the corresponding age categories. The native white group, on the other hand, showed that 36 per cent of all female arrests fell into the 35 plus age category as against only 23 per cent of all male arrests.[10]

A similar picture can be gained from analysis of the criminal statistics for England and Wales. In 1930, for instance, women 40 years of age and over represented 25.6 per cent of all women found guilty in court; however, men in the same age group contributed only 15.4 per cent of all the men found so guilty. The corresponding figures for 1935 are 26.4 per cent (female) and 12 per cent (male).[11]

For Austria, Hugo Herz observed that in his material for the year 1899 the number of convicted women in the age bracket 40-60 was proportionately higher than the number of men convicted.[12]

For Germany, Hugo Hoegel tested the official statistical material for the period 1886-95 by computing the sex differentials between the male and female convictions by age groups. He found a relatively much slower decline in female criminality than in the criminality of men. In the age group 21-25, for instance, he found that male convictions were 7.5 times as frequent as the female convictions; in the age group 40-50, however, he found them to be only 3.3 times as frequent.[13]

A study of the sex ratios apparent in Polish criminal statistics followed a slightly different method and arrived at substantially the same result. In that study the ratio of female per 100 male convictions was computed by age groups on the basis of the average annual convictions for the period 1924-28. This method does not require the cumbersome process of rethinking the numerical values of the index figures into inverse values of the criminal liability of the female sex and permits, therefore, a faster grasp of their meaning.

TABLE 24

SEX DIFFERENTIALS IN THE INCIDENCE OF MALE AND FEMALE CONVICTIONS, BY AGE GROUPS, POLAND, 1924-28*

Age	Incidence of Female Convictions per 100 Male Convictions
10-19	17.8
20-29	12.9
30-39	21.9
40-49	31.8
50-59	34.4
60	38.6

* Radzinowicz, *op. cit.*, p. 79.

Again the relatively low degree of female criminality in the age group of early maturity (21-29) and its relatively high degree in the more advanced age groups seem to indicate that the decline of female criminality in the years of later maturity is distinctly slower than the decline of male criminality in this age period.

Such index figures, however, have the weakness of using sex ratios which we have come to consider as distorted and badly misleading. For this reason, a definite statement regarding the question of the apparently slower decline of the criminality of women will have to be postponed until the phenomenon is tested by a more reliable method.

Retests.

We have arrived at the second part of our probing into the age liabilities of female crime, and it seems advisable now to retest the material as far as possible by one research method only and particularly by one which does not unnecessarily introduce the probability of distortions. This can be safeguarded by making comparisons of relatives which are confined to data referring to only one sex group. Such relatives are to be found in the proportionate concentrations of crime in the various age groups within the totals of the criminalities of either sex. One further precautionary measure, however, seems necessary. Differentials between male and female offense concentrations in the various age categories may be caused, not only by differentials in the relative frequency of crimes committed, but also by differentials in the actual numbers of men and women in the same age groups. A method must therefore be found which eliminates this potential source of error. In the following tabulations, the attempt is made to solve this problem by computing the proportionate concentrations of arrests and convictions on the basis, not of absolute incidence figures, but of crime ratios per 100,000's of the general population in each of the age categories used.

Thus, in order to arrive at a meaningful picture, a hypothetical population is set up in which every age group for which official criminal statistics permit the calculation of a crime rate is supposed to contain 100,000 persons. As compared with the actual frequency of people in these age groups, this is unrealistic, of course. For purposes of showing definite age liabilities, however, it furnishes a basis for a more searching comparison.

If we then compare on that basis the proportionate concentrations of male crime in the various age groups within the framework of male criminality with the proportionate concentrations of female crime in the various age groups within the framework of female criminality, we arrive at the following results.

The material for New York State presented in Table 25 indicates that the criminal liabilities of women from 21 up to 59 years of age are relatively higher than the criminal liabilities for men in this period. In addition, however, attention should be drawn to the fact that women 19 years of age show a higher liability than those 16-18 and those 20 years old.

The British material on indictable offenses is even more revealing if treated in the same fashion as shown in Table 26.

TABLE 25

PROPORTIONATE CONCENTRATIONS OF MAJOR OFFENSES, BY AGE AND SEX, AS
REFLECTED IN ARREST RATIOS PER 100,000, NEW YORK STATE, 1938*

Age	Male	Female
all ages	100%	100%
16-18	17.03	7.71
19	17.40	11.92
20	15.04	9.82
21-24	14.03	17.88
25-29	11.43	18.04
30-34	8.64	13.64
35-39	7.35	10.87
40-49	6.07	7.81
50-59	1.62	1.68
60	1.39	.63

* Based on State of New York, *Ninth Annual Report of the Commissioner
of Correction on Crime Statistics*, p. 458.

TABLE 26

PROPORTIONATE CONCENTRATIONS OF INDICTABLE OFFENSES, BY AGE AND SEX, AS
REFLECTED IN CONVICTION RATIOS PER 100,000, ENGLAND AND WALES, 1938*

Age	Male	Female
all ages	100%	100%
8	1.71	0.72
9	3.52	2.17
10	5.49	2.98
11	7.28	4.99
12	8.68	5.31
13	10.28	5.87
14	8.92	6.76
15	8.95	7.80
16	8.67	7.32
17	6.78	7.96
18	5.78	8.53
19	5.99	8.69
20	5.20	7.56
21-24	4.37	6.19
25-29	3.37	4.99
30-39	2.40	4.91
40-49	1.42	4.02
50-59	0.79	2.41
60	0.40	0.80

* Based on *Criminal Statistics, England and Wales, 1938* (London, 1940),
Appendix 3(A), p. xxxiii.

Table 26 shows the advantage of detailed age statistics. All
the problems in question, the later start, the later peak incidence,
the higher criminal liability of female adolescence, and the rela-

tively slower decline of the criminality of women with advancing years are clearly indicated.

Similar treatment of Belgian, Italian, and German statistics shows throughout the slower decline and, with one exception, also the later peak incidence of female criminality expressed in the relative proportionate concentrations of convictions by age and sex. Where the figures refer to sufficiently early age groups, they show also that the start of women in crime is slower before puberty than in the case of boys. For reasons of space only one set of these European data is presented in this fashion.

TABLE 27

PROPORTIONATE CONCENTRATIONS OF MAJOR OFFENSES, BY AGE AND SEX, AS REFLECTED IN CONVICTION RATIOS PER 100,000, GERMANY, 1886-95 AND 1929*

| | 1886-95 | | 1929 | |
Age	Male	Female	Male	Female
all ages	100%	100%	100%	100%
12-14	3.61	0.43	...	...
14-15	...	...	2.91	3.59
15-17	7.53	9.71	...	...
16-17	...	...	6.61	7.48
18-21	25.91	13.39	15.95	14.36
22-24	17.74	13.39	20.80	17.16
25-29	15.61	14.54	18.50	16.41
30-39	12.04	15.78	14.85	14.88
40-49	8.80	14.75	10.71	12.90
50-59	5.70	9.50	6.53	9.05
60-69	3.05	4.62	3.15	4.19

* Based on Roesner, "Alter und Straffälligkeit," *Handwörterbuch der Kriminologie*, pp. 26, 28.

The major points of this table are, of course, again the slow start of girls in crime before puberty and the relatively higher liability of women for crimes in the age brackets of maturity. It is also interesting to see that late puberty and early adolescence may produce relatively higher criminal liabilities for girls than for boys.

In summary, then, the whole material seems to suggest a pronounced delay in the rise, the peak incidence, and the decline of the crime rate as the distinctive characteristics of the age liabilities of women in crime. There is also some material indicative of a relatively high, if not higher, liability of women in puberty and adolescence, but the amount of available material in this respect is not equally satisfactory.

The general phenomenon of delay in the criminality of women becomes even more convincing if one bears in mind that most of the data on the ages of offenders are based on information offered by the offenders themselves and that many women are inclined to understate their age as soon as they have passed the mid-twenties. Of course, it could be claimed that the belief in a universal desire of women to appear as young as possible is only a jocular expression of male antagonism against the other sex. It deserves attention, however, that Frances A. Kellor, a pioneer in sociology, once cautioned that where she had an opportunity of learning the true age of a woman prisoner she found it was always more than the age given by the offender.[14] At any rate, it is certainly established that women pay for maturity a distinctly higher price in crime than do men.

This phenomenon of the comparative retardation of the female age liabilities in crime has aroused a certain amount of surprise. Deductive thinking could have led to the expectation that the general physiological and mental precocity of the female sex[15] would express itself also in an earlier development of the female crime curve, and Dora Melegari actually drew attention to this apparent inconsistency.[16] Closer analysis, however, shows that this seemingly contradictory phenomenon provides, in fact, a key to the understanding of some causative factors in female crime rather than an enigma. A detailed discussion of the factors which cause female criminality will be presented in a later part of this study. Still, two basic considerations may be pointed out at this stage of our investigation. (1) Women undergo in the years of maturity a number of physiological crises which do not occur in the maturation process of men. (2) Because of the greater protection of girls in our culture, maturity brings to women a more spectacular broadening of their life sphere and a correspondingly greater increase in criminal opportunities and temptations than it brings to men.

NOTES

[1] Reckless, *Criminal Behavior*, p. 106.
[2] Based on Home Office, *Criminal Statistics, England and Wales, 1930* (London, 1932), p. 58; *1935* (London, 1937), p. 58.
[3] J. H. Cassity, "Sociopsychiatric Aspects of Female Felons," *The Journal of Criminal Psychopathology*, III (1941-42), 603.
[4] Home Office, *Criminal Statistics, England and Wales, 1938* (London, 1940), Appendix 3(A), p. xxxiii.
[5] Jacquart, *op. cit.*, p. 73.
[6] Melegari, *op. cit.*, p. 530.
[7] Niceforo, *op. cit.*, p. 613.
[8] Ernst Roesner, "Alter und Straffälligkeit," *Handwörterbuch der Kriminologie*, pp. 26, 28.
[9] Herx, *op. cit.*, p. 27.
[10] Based on State of New York, *Eleventh Annual Report of the Commissioner of Correction on Crime Statistics*, p. 418.
[11] Based on Home Office, *Criminal Statistics, England and Wales, 1930* (London, 1932), p. 58; *1935* (London, 1937), p. 58.
[12] Herz, *op. cit.*, p. 289.
[13] Hoegel, *op. cit.*, p. 238.
[14] Kellor, "Psychological and Environmental Study of Women Criminals," *The American Journal of Sociology*, V (1900), 673.
[15] Scheinfeld, *op. cit.*, p. 48.
[16] Melegari, *op. cit.*, p. 530.

CHAPTER IX

PERSONAL CHARACTERISTICS OF FEMALE OFFENDERS: MARITAL STATUS, OCCUPATIONS, INTELLIGENCE, AND RACE

Following the plan of discussion indicated in the preceding chapter, the material presented here will deal with the available information on the conjugal conditions, the occupational pursuits, the intelligence level, and the race of female offenders. This information is largely unsatisfactory because of a great lack of meaningful material regarding most of these aspects of female crime. More research seems to be needed here than for any other of the questions so far discussed.

Marital Status.

The relationship between marital status and criminality seems to be different for women and men. Scientific opinion is not unanimous in this respect, but an impressive number of scholars have found that the unmarried seem to contribute a relatively greater share to the criminality of men than those in the same category contribute to the criminality of women. In other words, married offenders appear to be more frequent among women than among men.[1] The much smaller number of investigators who have come to express a different opinion are mostly scholars who have studied material from Eastern Europe.[2] Thus, there seems to exist a cultural differential in this respect, and this suggests that the influence of marriage upon the criminality of women is not so strong a factor as to appear in all sets of data independent of variables according to the source of the material.

As has always been the case in the presentation of the material so far, statistical problems have again to be considered. Several authors have pointed out that a breakdown of offender samples according to marital status only may be misleading, because singleness, marriage, and widowhood are roughly correlated with age, and different degrees of concentration of criminals in these various marital status groups may be reflections of age rather than of the civil status.[3] This consideration makes it necessary to disregard all sets of data which do not give a simultaneous age breakdown or a comparison with the respective proportions of the single, married, and widowed in the general population, and results, therefore, in a substantial curtailment of the material available for analysis. It forces us, for instance, to exclude the marital status data in the yearly reports of the United States Bureau of the Census on prisoners and the two great French government reports on criminal justice[4] from our presentation although they have been mentioned in the literature in this respect.

Furthermore, it has to be considered that the widowed and the divorced do not belong in the same category because they represent different social phenomena. Unfortunately, however, the European criminal statistics frequently lump these two groups together,[5] and thereby deprive the data of their sociological value.

Finally, it would be of great interest to find out how the criminal liabilities of the various civil status groups distribute themselves among the major groups of crime, if not among the individual offense types. Such material, however, has come to the attention of the writer only for the United States, Germany, and Belgium,[6] and because of its relative scarcity will be presented in a later connection where the emphasis is not confined to purely statistical evidence.

As long as we then want to adhere to the principal of international statistical comparisons, the meaningful material available seems to reduce itself to the following data regarding the apparent influence of marriage on crime in general.

Investigation of the civil status of criminals in the United States is handicapped by a great dearth of satisfactory official data. The Uniform Crime Reports give no material whatsoever

in this respect, and the reports of the Bureau of the Census—
as already mentioned—have no age breakdowns in combination
with their civil status analyses. Only one special study of the
Bureau of the Census made an exception in this respect and reported the following figures.

TABLE 28

COMMITMENTS TO PRISONS AND REFORMATORIES DURING THE FIRST SIX MONTHS
OF 1923, PER 100,000 IN THE GENERAL POPULATION, BY SEX, AGE,
AND MARITAL STATUS*

Age	Male		Female	
	Single	Married	Single	Married
all ages	72.0	31.6	4.0	2.9
15-24	73.1	100.2	4.7	7.9
15-19	52.5	158.8	3.9	11.2
20-24	102.5	95.8	6.4	7.1
25-34	81.9	49.2	3.4	3.1
35-44	74.0	27.9	1.6	2.0
45	33.5	11.6	—a	0.6

* Based on U. S. Bureau of the Census, *The Prisoner's Antecedents* (Wash-
ington, 1929), p. 24; also reproduced by Walter A. Lunden, *Statistics on Crime
and Criminals*, p. 39.
a Ratio not shown, the number of prisoners being insignificant.

According to these figures, married male prisoners seem to have
higher general crime rates than have single male prisoners only
in the age group 15-19 and have significantly lower rates in all
other age groups. Married female prisoners, however, have higher
rates than have the single female prisoners in all age groups except between 25 and 34 years and in the latter the differential
is comparatively insignificant.

Italian data for the years 1897 to 1900 show basically the same
differential although it is not quite so pronounced as in the
American material presented above. According to them, there
was a preponderance of criminality on the part of the married
over the single male offenders only in the age group 18-25 while
the criminality of the married women exceeded that of the single
women in the age group 14 to 25 and from 50 years of age up.[7]

In Austria, a combined sex, age, and marital status breakdown
was made for the years 1902 and 1903. The material, however,
was again restricted to convictions for serious crimes (*Verbrechen*). Thus, it does not reflect a cross section of the criminal-

ity of either sex. It must furthermore be kept in mind that the Austrian population at that period was composed of different ethnic and cultural groups including a strong Slavic element. At any rate, the unfavorable influence of marriage upon the criminality of women appears there less clearly than in the data for the United States and Italy, but it is still expressed to a certain degree. While in the male group the married never exceeded the single, in the female group the married did so, at least after age 50, and after age 30 their rates were relatively higher than those of the married males.[8]

The most detailed investigations of the correlation between the extent of crime and the civil status of the offenders have been made in Germany. The pioneer in this type of research was Friedrich Prinzing, whose data and findings have been widely quoted in the literature.[9]

TABLE 29

CONVICTION RATES FOR MAJOR OFFENSES (*Verbrechen* AND *Vergehen*) PER 100,000 IN THE GENERAL POPULATION, ACCORDING TO SEX, AGE, AND MARITAL STATUS, GERMANY, 1882-93*

| | | Male | | Female | |
Age		Single	Married	Single	Married
18- under 21		2,994.5	6,413.0	415.2	602.5
21- " 25		3,107.0	3,566.3	417.5	469.9
25- " 30		2,950.9	2,504.7	440.7	454.5
30- " 40		2,880.9	1,961.2	446.2	500.0
40- " 50		2,205.7	1,487.8	334.7	468.2
50- " 60		1,241.9	1,009.8	221.5	299.5
60		494.6	490.1	102.2	133.4

* Based on Prinzing, "Der Einfluss der Ehe auf die Kriminalität des Mannes, *Zeitschrift für Sozialwissenschaft*, II, Alte Folge (1899), 42, and "Die Erhöhung der Kriminalität des Weibes durch die Ehe," p. 437.

This table speaks for itself and does not require any elaboration. Prinzing's work was carried on by Hans Krille, who presented civil status figures for women offenders during the twenty-year period 1893-1902 and 1903-12 (Table 30).

For Belgium, rates similar to those shown for the other countries have not been worked up. At least, crime rates of the single and the married for corresponding age groups have not come

TABLE 30

Conviction Rates for Major Offenses (*Verbrechen* and *Vergehen*) of Female Offenders per 100,000 Women in the General Population, According to Age and Marital Status, Germany, 1893-1912*

Age	1893-1902		1903-12	
	Single	Married	Single	Married
21- under 25	406	426	377	472
25- " 30	429	441	392	451
30- " 40	423	504	387	482
40- " 50	292	468	284	457
50- " 60	185	305	169	290

* Based on Krille, *op. cit.*, p. 14.

to the attention of the writer. The official report on criminal statistics for the year 1900, however, tried to clarify the relationship between marital status and crime by calculating the ratios between the unmarried and the married of either sex in the general population and by comparing them with the ratios of the unmarried and the married in the respective sex groups of convicted offenders. By this procedure, it was found that if the proportion of the unmarried and the married (including widowed and divorced persons) in the general population had been correctly reflected in the conviction figures, there should have been 455 married men in each 1,000 men convicted and 580 married women in each 1,000 women convicted. Actually the conviction figures showed 442 married men and 728 married women in each 1,000 offenders of the respective sex. On that basis the official report concluded that the unfavorable influence of marriage upon the criminality of women could not be questioned.[10]

There is, however, one set of data reported in the literature which is clearly contradictory to the general character of the material presented regarding this question.

TABLE 31

Conviction Rates per 100,000 Persons in the General Population, According to Sex, Age, and Marital Status, Poland, 1924-28*

Age	Male		Female	
	Single	Married	Single	Married
20-24	1,461.8	1,530.0	199.7	131.9
25-29	1,284.9	1,331.0	325.5	144.7
30-39	1,053.4	827.7	426.9	152.8
40-49	871.3	518.3	300.7	138.9
50	459.4	311.9	175.1	102.1

* Based on Radzinowicz, *op. cit.*, p. 82.

This table seems to suggest that in Poland married women have a much lower criminality than the single women. It is now interesting to recall that the only other set of data which seemed to indicate at least in the majority of age groups a lesser criminality of the married than of the single women were the Austrian figures for 1902 and 1903, i.e., data for a period in which Austria included Galicia, a Polish province which later became incorporated into the newly established Poland as a result of World War I. This raises the interesting question whether marriage for Polish women presents a situation so different from that which it implies for the women of Central Europe and America that this difference expresses itself even in crime. This question cannot be answered with the material available, but it should be noted that among Polish peasants it was considered the husband's duty not to let his wife do any hired work, if he could possibly manage to support her.[11]

In general, however, the material available in the literature suggests that at least in our culture the criminal liability of married women is, independent of age, higher than the criminal liability of single women. Research into the causative factors of female crime will have to be mindful of this statistical observation.

Occupation.

The influence of occupational pursuits upon the criminality of women has been investigated to a much less satisfactory degree, but the existing material includes two findings which appear fairly convincing: that the criminal liability of women working in domestic service seems to be relatively high and that of women working in factories relatively low.

For the United States, it has been pointed out that among female prisoners the largest groups seem to come from domestic or other personal services. At the turn of the century, a study of 1,451 prisoners at Blackwell Island found 1,298 domestics, 125 housekeepers, and the remainder composed of laundresses, laborers, seamstresses, dressmakers, cooks, and peddlers.[12] About ten years later, an investigation of women lawbreakers taken mainly from the manufacturing states of the Union showed 77.5 per cent of the offenders engaged in domestic and personal services

as against only 40.4 per cent participation of women wage earners of 16 years and over in these occupations. Women in manufacturing and mechanical pursuits, however, represented only
16.7 per cent of the offenders against a 24.8 per cent participation
in the total of women wage earners.[13]

Austrian statistics which have been quoted in the literature
show a similar relationship between the criminal liabilities of
women in these two occupational groups. For the two-year span
1900-1901, the statistics of serious offenses (*Verbrechen*) indicated that female domestics had a crime rate of 21 per 100,000,
while women who worked in factories had a corresponding crime
rate of only 9 per 100,000.[14]

French authors and the Belgian De Ryckère have complained
repeatedly about the great criminal liability of female domestics.
Unfortunately, their material, although highly suggestive in other
ways, contains no satisfactory statistics in this respect.[15] The merit
of these authors lies more in emphasizing the highly masked
character of the offenses of domestics than in showing convincingly that even so statistics indicate a relatively high criminal
liability of women in this occupational group. In other words,
their work has added significance to the statistical data produced by the American and Austrian investigators rather than
producing additional data of the same nature.

Finally, it may be of interest that the high criminal liability
of female domestics has also been reported by a South American
author in a study of social factors in the female criminality of
Chile.[16]

To the author's knowledge, opposition to the opinion of the
remarkably high participation of domestics in female crime has
only been expressed by Aschaffenburg and Parmelee. However,
the tabulation of the occupations of German offenders upon
which their conclusions have been based had no sex breakdown,
and the heavy participation of the male population in agricul-
ture, manufacturing, and commerce must have greatly affected
the appearance of the various occupational percentages.[17]

Considering the data shown by official criminal statistics which
permit a breakdown by occupation as well as sex, the findings
of the special American investigations regarding this question,

and the exceptional degree to which this particular criminality of women is masked, there can be little doubt that the criminal liability of women in domestic service is very high.

The relatively low criminality of women working in factories, on the other hand, is further substantiated by Italian data.

TABLE 32

CONVICTION RATES OF WOMEN EMPLOYEES PER 100,000 PERSONS IN THE CORRESPONDING POPULATION BY OCCUPATION, ITALY, 1891-95*

Occupation	Conviction Rate
Manufacturing	193.38
Seamstresses, dressmakers, milliners	138.15
Sale of food and fuel	511.49
Other kinds of commerce	3,113.34

* Based on Bonger, *Criminality and Economic Conditions*, p. 447.

It should be noted that these figures do not include a special category for domestics. They show, on the other hand, a very high liability of women employed in commerce. The latter, however, is not supported by material from other countries. Actually, the American data in Mary Conyngton's study would seem to indicate the opposite. According to these data women engaged in commerce formed only 3.31 per cent of the women offenders who worked for wages while at that time women so engaged formed 10 per cent of the female wage earners in the United States population.[18] So far, then, nothing definite can be said regarding the relative criminal liability of this occupational group. Further research will be necessary to amplify our knowledge regarding the correlations between the occupational pursuits of women and female crime beyond the recognition of the heavy criminal liability of women in domestic and personal service and the apparently low rate of female factory workers.

Intelligence.

Compared with the results achieved, an undue amount of research effort has been spent on comparisons between the average intelligence levels of prisoners and those of the general population. This is equally true for women as it is for men.

Intelligence testing of women offenders has been going on since the beginning of this century, and the findings have differed considerably among each other. To name only a few of the better-known investigators, we find the following array of opinions. Augusta F. Bronner found that the delinquent girls of her study group were no more lacking in intelligence enabling them to earn a livelihood in legitimate vocations than the girls in her control group who succeeded in doing so.[19] According to Mabel Ruth Fernald and her collaborators, the women offenders in their study were "somewhat" inferior to the general population, and the most the authors were prepared to say was that "other things being equal there is apparently a greater presumption in favor of delinquency in a group of women who are below the average in intelligence than in a group above the average."[20] Jean Weidensall, Edith R. Spaulding, Georgiana S. Mendenhall, and the Gluecks, however, found a high incidence of defective intelligence among the members of their study groups.[21]

More significant results have been produced by Leslie Day Zeleny, who drew attention to the apparent existence of a differential in average mentality between male and female prisoners. He attempted to integrate a large number of the more important psychometric studies by reworking the data according to certain unifying principles. In doing so, he found that the variations which existed among these studies were partly due to a lack of realization that female prisoners showed higher percentages of mental defectiveness among their numbers than did male prisoners.

TABLE 33

MENTAL INFERIORITY RATIOS OF CRIMINALS TO NONCRIMINALS, BY SEX*

Type of Criminals	Ratio
Male juvenile delinquents	1.8 : 1
Female juvenile delinquents	2.7 : 1
Male adult criminals	1.3 : 1
Female adult criminals	2.8 : 1

* Based on Zeleny, "Feeble-Mindedness and Criminal Conduct," *The American Journal of Sociology*, XXXVIII (1932-33), 574.

The suggestive character of these ratios, however, must not lead to a neglect of the fact that according to Zeleny's estimates, only 3.2 per cent of the male and only 5.9 per cent of the female criminal population were below the upper limit of feeble-mindedness and that while these estimates are higher than the estimates of feeble-mindedness in the general population, they are numerically far too small to attribute to feeble-mindedness any great importance in the causation of criminal behavior.[22]

Related to these findings regarding a sex differential in the intelligence level between men and women offenders are various indications that mental defectiveness is more pronounced among certain types of female offenders than among others. Once more, it was the keenness of Frances A. Kellor's observations which noticed a meaningful aspect of female crime. As early as 1900 she reported a marked difference in the degree of mental defectiveness between prostitutes and other female offenders, the former being more defective than the latter.[23] Her observation was supported by a later study of 100 individuals arrested only for offenses against chastity. That study showed a proportion of 30 per cent feeble-mindedness among the offenders.[24] It was further confirmed by Clarence H. Growdon, who pointed out that the earliest studies of the mentalities of women offenders had been made in jails, workhouses, and similar institutions with a showing of very low intelligence scores, while later studies dealt more with women in penitentiaries and indicated that the intelligence of the offenders found in these institutions was higher than the earlier studies would have led him to expect.[25]

In summary, it can be said that the intelligence factor seems to play a very small role in the criminality of either sex and that the apparently somewhat unfavorable differential for women may be largely due to the low intelligence level of prostitutes. Intelligence or lack of intelligence, however, may be a factor in the nature of the offense committed.

Race.

The existing material on the race factor in female crime is comparatively scarce, and its analysis reveals only three major opinions: (1) negro women are said to have a much higher criminality than white women; (2) they are believed to surpass the criminality of white women to a greater degree than negro men seem to surpass the criminality of white men; and (3) their criminality appears to come closer to the criminality of negro men than the

116 THE CRIMINALITY OF WOMEN

criminality of white women does with regard to that of white men.[26]

All these impressions of quantitative relationships between negro crime and white crime are based on official criminal statistics and seem to follow from analyses of arrest as well as of commitment data.

New York State arrest data 1940 offer, for instance, the following picture:

TABLE 34

ARREST RATIOS PER 100,000 PERSONS IN THE GENERAL POPULATION, ACCORDING TO SEX AND RACE, NEW YORK STATE, 1940*

Sex and Race	Ratio
White female	11.7
Negro female	181.1
White male	263.5
Negro male	1,890.3

* Based on New York State, *Eleventh Annual Report of the Commissioner of Correction on Crime Statistics,* pp. 418-19; *Sixteenth Census of the United States: 1940, Population,* II, Part 5, p. 17. This table excludes persons under 20 years of age because of incompatibility between the age breakdowns in the statistical sources.

Simple inspection of these crime rates of female offenders as well as calculation of the race differentials in the two sex groups and of the sex differentials in the two race groups actually seems to bear out the quantitative relationships recorded in the literature. Certainly the arrest rate of negro women is much higher than that of white women. Actually it is 15.5 times higher. The arrest rate of negro men, however, is only 7.2 times that of white men. Finally, the arrest rate of negro women is about 10 per cent of the arrest rate of negro men while the arrest rate of white women is less than 5 per cent of the arrest rate of white men.

Commitment data give similar impressions and may actually be preferable in this respect because antinegro bias on the part of white police officers leads to a much larger number of unjustified arrests of negroes than of white persons.[27]

United States data for 1940 (Table 35) show the ratio of negro women received in state and federal prisons to be 5.8 times as high as the commitment rate of white women. The commitment rate of negro men is only four times higher than the

TABLE 35

RATIOS OF PRISONERS RECEIVED FROM COURTS BY STATE AND FEDERAL PRISONS,
PER 100,000 PERSONS 15 YEARS AND OLDER IN THE GENERAL POPULATION,
ACCORDING TO SEX AND RACE, 1940*

Sex and Race	Ratio
White female	3.6
Negro female	20.9
White male	95.3
Negro male	384.7

* Based on U. S. Bureau of the Census, *Prisoners—1940*, pp. 7-8; *Sixteenth Census of the United States: 1940, Population*, II, Part 1, p. 22. Prisoners under 15 years could not be excluded in the actual computation of these ratios because their numbers are not broken down by race in the Census reports; their total incidence, however, is negligible (18 males and 1 female).

commitment rate of white men. The commitments of white women represent only 4 per cent of the number of commitments of white men, and the commitments of negro women 5.3 per cent of the commitment total of negro men. In other words, negro women approach the commitment frequency of negro men more closely than white women approach the commitment frequency of white men. The degree to which they do so, however, is less pronounced than the degree to which their arrests approach negro male arrests.

Thus, the apparent and legal criminality of negro women as reflected in arrest and commitment data seem to reveal basically the same quantitative relationships to the criminality of white women and to the criminality of men, but to a different degree.

An analysis by Sutherland of commitment data for the year 1923 has thrown light on the reasons of this differential. In that year, commitments of negro women to prisons and reformatories were only 4.6 times as numerous as the commitments of white women to these institutions, while the commitments of negro women to jails and workhouses occurred 10.3 times as frequently as the commitments of white women.[28] Since the data presented in Table 35 refer only to commitments to state and federal prisons, commitments of negro women to jails and workhouses are not reflected in the apparent differential. They are, however, reflected although exaggeratedly in arrest data.

Sutherland's opinion regarding the greater frequency of the commitments of negro women to institutions of the jail and workhouse type has received further corroboration from investigations regarding the nature of the offenses for which they are most frequently arrested. A study of social and economic conditions in Harlem in 1935 made by E. Franklin Frazier revealed that approximately 80 per cent of the negro women arrested were charged with sex offenses.[29] Another more recent study of the conditions in Harlem confirmed this for 1942. It revealed that 54 per cent of the women arrested for prostitution in New York City were negroes and that the rate for the latter was ten times that for white women.[30]

All these impressions regarding the quantitative aspects of female criminality among negroes have to be received with a great deal of caution. Hans von Hentig has shown that at least a part of the impression that negro women have a higher criminality than white women is due to the fact that the population distribution with regard to relatively crime-free ages and relatively crime-disposed ages is more favorable in the white groups.[31] Furthermore, discrimination in law enforcement against colored women may well distort the picture. As far as imprisonment and releases from prisons are concerned, this can hardly be doubted. Many years ago, Frances A. Kellor pointed out that in the South the pardoning power of the executives was not equally applied to white and negro women. White women were generally pardoned because prison conditions were considered unfit for them but no such consideration was shown to negro women.[32] Such differential treatment may still exist. It may also be effective in commitment practices and not only in the South. It may even more influence the arrest figures. The courtesy which our law enforcement officers show to women offenders in a certain reluctance to arrest may be more pronounced in the case of white than in the case of negro women. Finally, we have to consider to what degree the criminality of white women is masked by their social roles and conduct norms in our culture. Much closer analysis than has been done so far would be necessary with regard to the influence of the roles and conduct norms for negro women, before it would be permissible to assume that the female criminality of both races is equally masked. The social position of the negro woman seems to be much freer than that of the white woman.

Therefore, it may well be that her ways of committing crimes are more accessible to discovery than those which white women employ. More research will be necessary before the relative higher criminal liability of negro women can be accepted as an established fact and subjected to causational analysis.

NOTES

1 Best, *op. cit.*, pp. 227-28; Parmelee, *op. cit.*, pp. 238-39; Wood and Waite, *op. cit.*, p. 252; Gillin, *op. cit.*, p. 58; Sutherland, *op. cit.*, 3rd. ed., p. 171; Kellor, "Criminal Sociology—Criminality among Women," *Arena*, XXIII (1900), 519; Conyngton, *op. cit.*, pp. 24-26; L. Bodio, "Rapport sur la méthode du bulletin individuel appliquée à la statistique judiciaire pénale en Italie depuis l'année 1890," *Bulletin de l'Institut International de Statistique*, XII (1900), 373; Lombroso, *op. cit.*, p. 189; Melegari, *op. cit.*, p. 531; Bonger, *Crime and Economic Conditions*, p. 461; Prinzing, "Die Erhöhung der Kriminalität des Weibes durch die Ehe" in toto and "Soziale Faktoren der Kriminalität," *Zeitschrift für die Gesamte Strafrechtswissenschaft*, XXII (1902), 554, 558; Liepmann, *op. cit.*, p. 133; Schmitz, *op. cit.*, p. 11.

2 Colajanni, *op. cit.*, p. 112; M. Minovici, "Remarques sur la Criminalité Féminine en Roumanie," *Archives d'Anthropologie Criminelle*, XXII (1907), 571; Arnold Wadler, *Die Verbrechensbewegung im östlichen Europa*, I (Die Kriminalität der Balkanländer), p. 131; Radzinowicz, *op. cit.*, p. 82.

3 Parmelee, *op. cit.*, p. 237; Best, *op. cit.*, p. 228; Sutherland, *op. cit.*, 3rd ed., p. 171; Wood and Waite, *op. cit.*, p. 252; Hoegel, *op. cit.*, pp. 247-48; Von Mayr, *op. cit.*, p. 802.

4 U. S. Bureau of the Census, *Prisoners in State and Federal Prisons and Reformatories 1945*, pp. 28-30, and the corresponding material in the earlier issues; *Compte General de l'Administration de la Justice Criminelle pendant l'Année 1880*, p. xxx; *Compte General de la Justice Criminelle pendant l'Année 1900*, "Rapport au Président de la Republique sur l'Administration Criminelle en France de 1881 à 1900," p. xxiii.

5 Von Mayr, *op. cit.*, p. 809; Aschaffenburg, *op. cit.*, pp. 164-65; Jacquart, *op. cit.*, p. 80.

6 Aschaffenburg, *op. cit.*, pp. 164-65; Prinzing, "Die Erhöhung der Kriminalität des Weibes durch die Ehe," pp. 438 ff; Krille, *op. cit.*, pp. 16 ff; Jacquart, *op. cit.*, p. 82; Conyngton, *op. cit.*, p. 25.

7 Von Mayr, *op. cit.*, p. 810.

8 *Ibid.*, p. 809.

9 Aschaffenburg, *op. cit.*, pp. 164-65; Parmelee, *op. cit.*, p. 238; Von Mayr, *op. cit.*, pp. 806-7; Roesner, "Familienstand," *Handwörterbuch der Kriminologie*, I (1932), 399, 404-6.

10 Based on Jacquart, *op. cit.*, pp. 81-82.

11 William I. Thomas and Florian Znaniecki, *The Polish Peasant in Europe and America*, I, p. 90.

12 Kellor, "Psychological and Environmental Study of Women Criminals," p. 675.

13 Conyngton, *op. cit.*, p. 29.

14 E. Hurwicz, "Kriminalität und Prostitution der weiblichen Dienstboten," *Archiv für Kriminal-Anthropologie*, LXV (1916), 195; see for similar data regarding the year 1899, Herz, *op. cit.*, p. 294.

[15] Proal, *op. cit.*, p. 224; Armand Corre, *Crime et Suicide*, p. 515; De Ryckère, *La Servante Criminelle*, p. 22.

[16] F. Klimpel Alvarado, "Factores sociales de la delinquencia femenina en Chile," *Rev. Psiquiat. Crim.*, Buenos Aires, VII (1942), 113-28.

[17] Aschaffenburg, *op. cit.*, pp. 66-67; Parmelee, *op. cit.*, p. 83.

[18] Conyngton, *op. cit.*, p. 29.

[19] Bronner, *op. cit.*, p. 86.

[20] Fernald *et al.*, *op. cit.*, p. 527.

[21] Jean Weidensall, *The Mentality of the Criminal Woman*, p. 269; Spaulding, "The Results of Mental and Physical Examinations of Four Hundred Women Offenders—With Particular Reference to Their Treatment During Commitment," p. 715; Georgiana S. Mendenhall, "A Study of Behavior Problems," *The Psychological Clinic*, XXI (1932-33), 85-86; Sheldon and Eleanor T. Glueck, *op. cit.*, p. 192.

[22] Zeleny, *op. cit.*, p. 576; Reckless, *Criminal Behavior*, p. 204.

[23] Kellor, "Psychological and Environmental Study of Women Criminals," p. 543.

[24] V. V. Anderson, "The Immoral Woman as Seen in Court," *Journal of the American Institute of Criminal Law and Criminology*, VIII (1917-18), 904.

[25] Clarence H. Growdon, "The Mental Status of Reformatory Women," *Journal of the American Institute of Criminal Law and Criminology*, XXII (1931-32), 196.

[26] Von Hentig, "The Criminality of the Colored Woman," *University of Colorado Studies*, Series C, I, No. 3 (1942), 233; Best, *op. cit.*, p. 230; Haynes, *op. cit.*, p. 85; Sutherland, *op. cit.*, 3rd ed., pp. 120-21; Taft, *op. cit.*, p. 88; Gillin, *op. cit.*, p. 56; Bonger, *Race and Crime*, p. 43.

[27] Myrdal, *op. cit.*, II, 970.

[28] Sutherland, *op. cit.*, 2nd ed. (1934), pp. 110-11.

[29] The Mayor's Commission on Conditions in Harlem, *The Negro in Harlem: A Report on Social and Economic Conditions Responsible for the Outbreak of March 19, 1935*, pp. 97-99, quoted by Myrdal, *op. cit.*, II, 974.

[30] New York City Welfare Council, *Report of the Sub-Committee on Crime and Delinquency of the City-Wide Citizens' Committee on Harlem* (New York, 1942), p. 5, quoted by Myrdal, *ibid.*

[31] Von Hentig, "The Criminality of the Colored Woman," p. 239.

[32] Kellor, "The Criminal Negro," *Arena*, XXV (1907), 312.

CHAPTER X

BIOLOGICAL FACTORS IN FEMALE CRIME

After the presentation of the general appearance of female crime as a preliminary to the study of its causation, attention will now be given to the latter. Material on those antecedents or probable conditions of criminal conduct which we may call in a general sense the causes of female crime[1] has been contributed by scientists in various fields. It has come from criminologists, sociologists, and psychologists, as well as from physiologists, gynecologists, psychiatrists, and psychoanalysts. As in the study of all types of behavior, however, the factors which have been discussed resolve themselves upon closer analysis into two groups, those of a biological and those of a social nature. It will be necessary, therefore, to draw upon all these various disciplines for material, but its organization can be meaningfully arranged only under the two headings of biological and social factors.

Logically, the causational analysis of the criminality of an offender group which is defined on a biological basis has to start with a discussion of the apparent relationships between the biological characteristics of the offenders and crime. It should be kept in mind, however, that the biological factors which seem to have a bearing on female crime do so mostly in their interaction with social factors and that correspondingly an adequate understanding of the social factors in female crime can be achieved only if they are considered with due regard to the biological characteristics of the offender group. The division of the material in biological and social factors indicates, therefore, more points of departure and degrees of emphasis than a clear-cut division of the material.

Before presenting material along these lines, however, a change

121

in the research technique so far pursued and a limitation in the material analyzed require explanation.

As long as the investigation was purely statistical, the unreliability of criminal statistics made it necessary to confine conclusions only to those characteristics of female crime which appeared in all or at least in the majority of data. In the investigation of the causational aspects the purely statistical method will be abandoned and reliance will be largely placed on nonstatistical analysis. Where nonstatistical information about the nature of a phenomenon suggests the relatively high criminal liability of women in certain offense types, spot statistics from only one country may be acceptable as supporting evidence.

Material which is to be found in the psychiatric literature will be omitted as far as it deals with mental conditions which would exclude legal responsibility; it will be used, however, to explain female behavior in general by inferring normality from study of the pathological. Although it is customary to include material on the criminally insane, or the insane criminal in the analyses of criminality in general, it is not proposed to do so here. Since this is not a study of the psychopathology of women, any extended discussion of the female insane criminal would be distinctly out of place. This study intends to reveal only what can be learned about the female criminal based exclusively upon the legal rather than the psychiatric criteria. Thus, while it may be interesting to pursue the psychopathology of female crime, this would lead too far afield from the topic of female crime in the legal sense, which delineates the area of this presentation.

Available and relevant information with respect to the influence of biological factors on female crime may now be presented. The material suggests three points of interest in this respect: (1) the influence of the sex differential in physical strength, (2) the effects of physiological development, and (3) the influence of the generative phases of women upon their criminality.

The Relative Physical Weakness of Women.

A strange disregard for technological realities has led various authors to the statement that women are incapable of committing certain crimes because of the lesser degree of physical strength which characterizes their sex. The prevalence of poisoners among female murderers, the frequency of children among the victims of women offenders, and their apparently low degree of participation in property crimes with violence have been explained on this basis.[2]

Here a cultural stereotype is obviously at work. That a woman should be too weak to pull the trigger of a gun or to handle burglar's tools but be strong enough to do menial work in the house, fields, and factories does not seem plausible today. What may have made sense in times when male criminals used the sword or similar crude and heavy mechanical devices has lost its technical validity in a period in which physical strength has become less and less necessary in the handling of mechanical tools. It seems rather that the roles of women and the stereotypes of female behavior characteristic of our culture furnish the explanation of the types of participation of our female offenders in crime. With us woman is not a bearer of arms, and until recently she has not been handling mechanical tools outside of her traditional sphere. The work of the warrior or the locksmith, the two professions after which male murderers, robbers, and burglars largely pattern their modi operandi are, therefore, outside her normal sphere and consequently not reflected in the ways in which she commits her crimes. Significantly the female murderers of peasant stock in the Tarnowsky material sometimes used the hatchet in their crimes, a tool which they handled in everyday life.[3]

It seems reasonable, therefore, to accept Luke Owen Pike's conclusion that at the present the relative physical weakness of women furnishes at best only an indirect explanation of the specificity of female crime, namely, in so far as it was the basis for the assignment of certain social roles and the basis for the denial of others to women.[4] Today, it is this role assignment and not physical necessity which channelizes their criminal behavior into certain directions and keeps it away from others.

Physiological Overdevelopment of Girls.

The American literature contains a few significant observations on the effect which precocious biological maturity has upon the delinquency of girls. Particularly Healy has drawn attention to the fact that physiological overdevelopment seems to play an important role among the causes underlying delinquency in girls. His charts of developmental conditions shown by weight correlated with age indicate a much greater incidence of delinquency among overdeveloped girls than among overdeveloped boys. The differential between physical development of boy and girl offenders was very pronounced. While the mentally normal boys were almost evenly distributed on each side of the curve of averages, 73 per cent of the mentally normal girls were reported as overweight for their age.[5]

Healy's findings were corroborated by the observations of various authors. Anne T. Bingham found that the group of 500 youthful female sex offenders whom she studied at Waverley House in New York was for all ages heavier than the estimated average weight of girls of corresponding age would have led her to expect.[6] A survey of 341 delinquent girls in a correctional school in California similarly showed overdevelopment in weight and height to be a characteristic of these offenders. The first impression of visitors at this school was generally one of surprise at the buxom vigor and strength of the majority of the girls.[7] Finally, Mabel Seagrave reported that among the streetwalkers and sex offenders who passed through the clinic with which she was connected in New York in 1910 and 1911, there was a preponderance of oversized and overweight girls. These girls who came from the ranks of the generally thin and ill-nourished children of the New York East Side resembled much more the prototype of the healthy farmer's daughter than that of the underprivileged child of the slums.[8]

Statutory rape legislation shows society's recognition of the dangers which the early appearance of sexual maturity in girls may cause in many instances. The penal law of the State of New York, for example, contains a section according to which "a person who perpetrates an act of sexual intercourse with a female, not his wife, under the age of eighteen years, under circumstances not amounting to rape in the first degree, is guilty of rape in the secondary degree." It might be interesting to note that before 1895 the age limit was actually only 16 years.[9] It is well known that most states have similar statutes which designate an age below which a girl's consent to sexual intercourse is legally invalid and does not free her partner of criminal responsibility for rape.[10]

It is now interesting to ask why physiological overdevelopment should cause juvenile delinquency more frequently among girls than among boys. Again the biological phenomenon taken by itself leaves us without a satisfactory answer. The nature of the delinquencies, however, which seem to be particularly correlated with the phenomenon of physiological overdevelopment furnishes an important clue. All these authors point out that it is particularly the girl sex delinquent who often shows such physiological precocity, and Healy saw the explanation of this phenomenon in the stress between the physiological urge and its mental management by an otherwise not sufficiently mature person.[11] On this basis, however, overdevelopment of the sex urge should, of course, drive a boy to such sex delinquencies just as much as a girl, and this seems not to be the case. In order to find the solution of this dilemma, it is necessary to consider the nature of our sex mores. The male has to be active while the female has to be passive. In the active attempt to find satisfaction for the sex urge, physiological precocity does not seem to help the boy very much but for the girl who has to wait until she is "propositioned," the appearance of sexual maturity furnishes opportunity for sex delinquencies which do not come the way of her normally developed age mates. We must conclude, therefore, that it is more the increase of opportunity resulting from the fact of overdevelopment in girls than the intensity of a premature sex urge which causes this differential in delinquency between male and female juveniles.[12]

The Generative Phases of Women.

Considerable interest has been extended by a number of authors to the question whether the procreative phases in the life of women have any bearing on their criminality, and the justification of such interest becomes immediately apparent, if one considers the results of the statistical investigations of the age factor in female crime. The fruitfulness of research into the possible conjunctions between menstruation, pregnancy, and the menopause on the one hand and female crime on the other is certainly suggested by the more even distribution of the criminal liabilities of women over the brackets of childbearing age. One word of warning, however, is in order. The mere fact that many female offenders commit their crimes in this period is not sufficient to indicate a causative relationship between the procreative phases and female crime. This has to be expected according to the characteristics of the universe from which the offender samples are drawn. Since most women menstruate between certain ages, become pregnant, and experience the climacteric, statistical probability makes it necessary that considerable numbers of female offenders should have committed their crimes while they were in one of these phases. The quest into the causes of female crime will be advanced only if it should be possible to show that either the nature of these phenomena or discovered statistical correlations suggest their significance for the causation of criminal behavior.

Although the function of menstruation is a normal biological phenomenon and seems to have very little, if any, adverse influence on the psychomotor performance capacities of women, the prevailing attitudes of the members of both sexes in all cultures have shown guilt and fear over it.[13] The psychological effects of these attitudes upon women have expressed themselves in special anxieties, suspicions, and superstitions regarding this normal biological occurrence. The resulting upsets of the mental balance in women have been noted over and over again since ancient times, and we find them mentioned in the works of Hippocrates as well as in the most recent editions of modern textbooks of gynecology.[14]

Psychoanalysis has done much for the interpretation of this phenomenon in our culture, or at least in that subculture from which its patients come. According to that type of explanation, the process of bleeding suggests the infliction of an injury, and children consider injury as a punishment for guilt. Because of rigidity in the early sex training of our children, their fear is particularly related to the region of the genitals. It is understandable that these apprehensions should lead them to interpret menstruation as such a punishment when they become aware of it. Furthermore, boys and girls may easily observe the unpleasant consequences of the regularly recurrent irritability of their mothers in their own sphere of life, because acts which go otherwise unnoticed are being punished at these periods. Either through their own curiosity or through carelessness of their mother, they soon come to connect these disturbing interludes in their own lives with the period of monthly bleeding or at least indisposition on the part of their mother. They thus form an attitude of apprehension with regard to this phenomenon which persists in later years. But in the course of their development menstruation assumes, of course, a much greater importance for girls than for boys. For the latter, it remains a symbol of danger and unpleasantness, but it stays at that. To the girls it actually happens and thus represents a confirmation of their anxiety. In addition they experience it as a narcissistic wound to their self-esteem. Setting the seal, so to speak, upon their womanhood, it destroys their hope ever to become a man, which until then they may have preserved, and intensifies any feeling of inferiority which they may have had about their sex. They are not permitted to forget this emotional experience during the whole period of their childbearing lives, being reminded of it every twenty-eight days. In this way menstruation becomes to women a symbol of injustice which arouses their desire for revenge. The onset of the first menstruation is for girls, therefore, in many instances an event of traumatic character. Whether prepared for it or not, they learn mostly that menstruation is something which they have to conceal and are frequently told that they should desist from activities and pleasures which they are otherwise at liberty to enjoy. The onset of puberty is consequently a more momentous and difficult event in the lives of girls than in the lives of boys.[15]

Psychological findings agree with this psychoanalytic theory. This appears particularly in a study of boys and girls between the ages of 9 and 19 years who were tested with the Woodworth-Mathews Questionnaire. This questionnaire consists of 100 questions dealing with four groups of symptoms related to (1) fear, worries, and perseverations; (2) physical difficulties; (3) unhappiness, unsocial, and antisocial moods; and (4) dreams, fantasies, and sleep disturbances. The test results indicated a median of 20 symptoms among the boys and of 25.5 symptoms among the girls. They showed further that while at age 10 the boys showed more neurotic symptoms than the girls, the sexes showed equal numbers of symptoms at age 11, and that from then on the girls exhibited a progressive increase of emotional instability until age 17, while the boys' symptoms oscillated between 11 and 13 years of age and decreased steadily after age 13.[16]

Against such a background of anxiety and fear in childhood and puberty, it is no wonder that the monthly recurrence of menstruation should cause a number of temporary psychological changes in women which have been classically summarized by Krafft-Ebing as follows:[17]

The menstruating woman has a claim to special consideration by the judge because she is at this period "unwell" and more or less psychologically disturbed. Abnormal irritability, attacks of melancholia, feelings of anxiety are common phenomena. Inability to get along with the husband and domestics, ill treatment of otherwise tenderly cared for children, emotional explosions, libelous acts, breach of peace, resisting authority, scenes of jealousy, craving of alcoholic beverages because of physical pains, neurotic and anxiety conditions are everyday experiences with innumerable individuals. [Author's translation.]

For the criminologist, it is also important to note that these psychological oscillations are not confined to the days of menstruation proper but may also be felt in the days immediately preceding and following,[18] although more frequently in the former than the latter.

The psychological connotations of this biological phenomenon in our culture would then certainly suggest that it should be a positive factor of considerable importance for female crime, and Aubry has expressed surprise that it has not received more consideration from this point of view.[19]

Unfortunately, it lies in the nature of this phenomenon that its relation to crime cannot be easily discovered. It lacks a connection with any age bracket used in criminal statistics and, furthermore, female offenders are very reticent regarding this fact. It has been observed during criminal trials that women would rather take the responsibility for an imputed offense than to admit that a bloodstain on their clothing or underwear originated from their own menstruation.[20] If women are so reluctant to use the fact of their menstruation for purposes of ridding themselves from an unjust accusation, it can easily be imagined how much their reluctance to refer to it must express itself in cases in which they have actually committed the offense. Often they do not even perceive how the fact that they had done so during the menstrual period could help them in the outcome of their case. Sometimes they feel rightly that the overcoming of their customary reticence regarding this phenomenon would not bring them any reward, because they are interrogated about it only after they find themselves in prison. It needs hardly any elaboration that this feeling of shame expresses itself even more in young girls who are still in the turmoil of puberty.

It is not surprising, therefore, that Healy and Burt have found only a comparatively small number of cases in which the behavior of their young female offenders could be related to the period of menstruation.[21]

Still, European authors have produced some material which suggests that a significant relationship actually exists. Lombroso found that among eighty women who were arrested for resistance against public officials, 71 were menstruating at the time of the offense.[22] Le Grand du Saulle observed that among 56 shoplifters in the department stores of Paris whom he had to examine, 35, i.e., 63 per cent, had committed the offense during the period of menstruation.[23] A similar observation is reported by Gudden, who found that in practically all cases of shoplifting which he investigated as an expert for the courts the offense had been committed at a time of menstruation.[24]

Case material suggests further that arson and homicides may be causally related to the stage of menstruation. This is illustrated by instances in which the offenses of persons who had committed them repeatedly could each be traced to the menstrual period of the offender.[25] In general, the Continental literature suggests that thefts and, most of all, shoplifting, arson, homicides, and resistance against public officials show a significant correlation between menstruation of the offender and the time at which the offense was committed.[26]

The turmoil of the onset of menstruation in the puberty of girls seems to be expressed particularly in relatively high incidences of false accusations and arson.[27] Perhaps the most instructive statistical material regarding arson in this respect is reported by Hoegel, as can be seen from the following table:

TABLE 36

INCIDENCE RATES OF FEMALE OFFENDERS CONVICTED OF ARSON, BY AGE, PER 10,000 WOMEN IN RESPECTIVE AGE GROUPS, GERMANY, 1886-95*

Age	Rate
12-15	.1
15-18	.1
18-21	.05
21-25	.03
25-30	.02
30-40	.03
40-50	.03
50-60	.02
60-70	.01
70	.01

* Based on Hoegel, *op. cit.*, p. 253.

Unfortunately, the German statistics do not contain a similar tabulation for false accusations, so no similar evidence can be presented regarding that offense.

It is interesting to note that the American material, although confirming the high criminal liability of girls with regard to false accusations, does not do so for arson. Figures produced by Healy in *The Individual Delinquent* show only 1 out of every 102 girls guilty of fire-setting as against 1 out of every 63 boys so guilty in his sample.[28] His findings are corroborated by a report for Manhattan, the Bronx, and Staten Island. According to this report, between 1933 and 1938 there were 72 charges of incendiarism against persons under 16 years of age, among whom there was only one girl.[29]

This apparent discrepancy between the German and American figures, however, does not speak against the crime-promoting influence of puberty in this respect, but shows only that predisposition cannot lead to criminal behavior without opportunity. The young girls who committed this crime in Germany were mostly in domestic service. Revenge, attempts to cover other crimes, and particularly homesickness have been believed to be the motive for their resorting to this offense.[30] On the other hand, the opinion has been expressed that these reported motives were only rationalizations of a much deeper motivation.[31] However that may have been, one may well ask whether the means of dealing with their emotional difficulties was not suggested to these girls by their daily routine tasks, which included the starting of fire in the stove of the household. On the other hand, one has to remember that in Chicago and New York there were hardly any pubescent girls who in the period in which these investigations took place were in domestic employment away from their homes, and that particularly the New York of the 1930's was a city from which coal stoves in kitchens had largely disappeared and with them the suggestion of a daily experience regarding this crime.

With regard to pregnancy, there are first of all certain offense types immediately connected with this procreative phase, namely, abortions and infanticides. We have already seen in the statistical section of this study to what extent abortions influence the quantity of female criminality. We have also found how much the modus operandi in infanticide is determined by the state of irritability and exhaustion after delivery, as well as by efforts of concealment. Furthermore, the psychological characteristics of pregnancy, such as unmotivated changes of moods, abnormal cravings and impulses, and temporary impairment of consciousness, point also in the direction of criminal causation.[32] One of these aspects deserves particular attention, the appearance of compelling cravings for certain things, especially foods unrelated to the normal eating routine of the person in question.[33]

With regard to shoplifters, it can easily be understood that such a physiologically based desire must lead to an increase of female thieves in a culture in which a highly developed sales technique is permanently at work to create ever new temptations. That the self-service system in food markets works especially in this direction needs no elaboration.

A special crime risk arises at the time when the pregnant person would under normal circumstances have her period of menstruation. The menstrual cycles do not lose their psychological impact immediately at the beginning of pregnancy but continue to influence the psychological state of women for at least several months afterwards.[34] Women are then under a twofold disturbance of their mental balance, and criminal behavior may result on that basis.[35]

In spite of all these considerations which would suggest pregnancy to be a crime-promoting factor, the literature does not contain any specific statistical study of an offender sample in this respect, and, therefore, it will be a task for further research to investigate the question of the correlation between pregnancy and female crime.

That the menopause is of great influence on women in biological, social, and psychological respects is generally accepted.[36] The menopausal syndrome includes the psychological characteristics of emotional instability, insomnia, depression of spirit, irritability, and anxiety attacks.[37]

These characteristics are largely ¬e to the meaning which women attribute to their climacteric. In our society in which the happiness and economic basis of many women, particularly in the middle classes, depend on marriage, anything which interferes with their roles as wives must be felt by them as a threat to their existence.[38] Then there is again the experience of narcissistic suffering.[39] Women often lose their sexual attractiveness and thereby one of their greatest assets in interpersonal relations, or at least they think they do. To make things worse, this process is accompanied by attacks of physiological ill feeling which, if menstruation should reoccur, may attain the character of a crisis. It is no wonder that the mental effect of this process should be increased irritability, impatience, restlessness, and irascibility.[40]

Actually some criminal statistics reveal a relatively high incidence of crime among women in the climacteric. This appears, for instance, in a comparison between the age distribution of all admissions to Michigan penal institutions in the period 1936 to 1938 and the age distribution of female admissions to these institutions in the same period. While only 25.9 per cent of all admissions fell into the age group of 35 to 54 years, 29.7 per cent of the female admissions fell into that age group.[41] Ohio figures for the year 1940 express this higher criminal liability of women in the 35 to 54 period even more strongly. In that year the age group 35 to 54 contributed 17.6 per cent of the commitments to the State Prison for Men but 35.9 per cent of the commitments of women to the Women's Reformatory of that state.[42] It is also possible to check whether the marital status makes a difference in criminality at this age and whether those offense types which specifically reflect the psychological characteristics of the menopause show a correspondingly high incidence at that period. German material particularly permits such an investigation.

In this respect it is interesting to note that a comparison between the crime rates for single and married women shows that the greatest difference in incidence between the two states occurs between 40 and 50. At this age the difference is most favorable for single women.[43] This seems to corroborate the opinion that the actual or merely imagined loss of her sexual attractiveness means more of a crisis for married women than for the single, as might have been expected.

As to special offense types characteristic of irritability and emotional disturbance, German statistics bear out the expectation of high incidence of female offenders at the critical age, particularly with regard to insults, perjury, and breach of peace. Actually, these offenses show peak incidence between 40 and 50 years, as can be seen from an inspection of the age rates in the following table.

TABLE 37

INCIDENCE RATES OF FEMALE OFFENDERS CONVICTED OF CRIMES OF IRRITABILITY, BY AGE, PER 10,000 WOMEN IN RESPECTIVE AGE GROUPS, GERMANY, 1886-95*

Age	Insults	Breach of Peace	Perjury
12-15	0.2	0.0	0.0
15-18	1.2	0.2	0.09
18-21	3.0	0.6	0.2
21-25	5.2	0.9	0.2
25-30	8.3	1.3	0.2
30-40	11.4	2.0	0.2
40-50	11.9	2.3	0.3
50-60	8.1	1.4	0.2
60-70	4.0	0.5	0.1
70	1.5	0.2	0.06

* Based on Hoegel, *op. cit.*, p. 253.

Another crime with a largely emotional basis—arson—does not show peak incidence but at least an increase of the crime rate between 30 and 50 years of age, as can be seen from the table presented earlier in this chapter (Table 36).

Peak incidence, however, in the period of menopause is further shown with regard to receiving stolen goods.

TABLE 38

INCIDENCE RATES OF FEMALE OFFENDERS CONVICTED OF RECEIVING STOLEN GOODS, BY AGE, PER 10,000 WOMEN IN RESPECTIVE AGE GROUPS, GERMANY, 1886-95*

Age	Rate
12-15	0.3
15-18	0.5
18-21	0.8
21-25	1.2
25-30	1.6
30-40	2.5
40-50	3.1
50-60	1.9
60-70	0.7
70	0.2

* Based on Hoegel, *op. cit.*, p. 253.

The coincidence of the peak rate with the age bracket of the menopause is apparent. However, since there is no other property crime in which the age of highest incidence is similar, the explanation already given that women of this age may in this way participate in the crimes of their sons who are reaching their age of greatest criminality against property is maintained. Again, it is the function of the mother and the housekeeper which seems to characterize and shape the criminal behavior of women in this respect.

That women in the menopause should have been noted also among shoplifters was to be expected. Particularly Leppmann reports having found them repeatedly among the cases which he had to examine.[44]

Understandable as it may be that the mental irritation of the menopause may make women more vulnerable from the point of view of temptation and suggestive as case material reported in the literature actually is, it seems advisable to apply caution in arriving at any conclusion regarding the influence of the menopause on shoplifting. With the number of female shoplifters in department stores there are bound to be among them women in the menopause, and there are no statistics available to probe further into this question.

In summary, it can be said that the material so far is more valuable regarding its suggestiveness than regarding its actual results. Carefully planned statistical investigations of offender samples with respect to the influence of menstruation and pregnancy upon female crime are largely missing, and it will be a task for further research to follow the leads which the material so far suggests.

NOTES

1 Sellin, *Culture Conflict and Crime*, p. 18.

2 Gross, *op. cit.*, p. 465; Minovici, *op. cit.*, p. 574; Parmelee, *op. cit.*, p. 240; Kellor, *Experimental Sociology*, p. 163; Sauer, *op. cit.*, II, 227, 335; Pollitz, *op. cit.*, pp. 27-28.

3 Tarnowsky, *op. cit.*, pp. 104-333.

4 Pike, *op. cit.*, p. 527.

5 Healy, *op. cit.*, p. 145.

6 Anne T. Bingham, "Determinants of Sex Delinquency in Adolescent Girls based on Intensive Studies of 500 Cases," *Journal of the American Institute of Criminal Law and Criminology*, XIII (1922-23), 543.

7 Julia Mathews, "A Survey of 341 Delinquent Girls in California," *The Journal of Delinquency*, VIII (1923), 206.

8 Mabel Seagrave, "Causes Underlying Sex Delinquencies in Young Girls," *Journal of Social Hygiene*, XII (1926), 526.

9 *Penal Law of New York*, Art. 180, § 2010, n. 1 (McKinney's, 1944).

10 Miller, *op. cit.*, p. 297.

11 Healy, *op. cit.*, p. 249.

12 Gillin, *op. cit.*, p. 84.

13 Edward Weiss and O. Spurgeon English, *Psychosomatic Medicine*, p. 352; Leta Stetter Hollingworth, *Functional Periodicity*, p. 93; Georgene H. Seward, *Sex and the Social Order*, p. 165.

14 Hippocrates, *Oeuvres Complètes*, transl. into French by E. Littré, V, pp. 553, 703, and VIII, pp. 275, 505; S. Icard, *La Femme pendant la Période Menstruelle*, pp. 41-42; Emil Novak, *Menstruation and Its Disorders*, p. 1; Mary Chadwick, *The Psychological Effects of Menstruation*, p. 1; Arthur Hale Curtis, *A Textbook of Gynecology*, 5th ed., p. 116; and many others.

15 Weiss and English, *op. cit.*, pp. 353-55; Chadwick, *op. cit.*, p. 43; Helene Deutsch, *Psychoanalyse der weiblichen Sexualfunktionen*, p. 27; Hanns Sachs, "The Wish to be a Man," *The International Journal of Psychoanalysis*, I (1920), 265-66.

16 Ellen Mathews, "A Study of the Emotional Stability in Children," *The Journal of Delinquency*, VIII (1923), 12, 21; also mentioned by Anne Anastasi, *Differential Psychology*, pp. 442-43.

17 Richard von Krafft-Ebing, *Psychosis Menstrualis*, pp. 93-94.

18 Healy, *op. cit.*, p. 628; Birnbaum, *Die psychopathischen Verbrecher*, p. 318; Charles Mazer and S. Leon Israel, *Diagnosis and Treatment of Menstrual Disorders and Sterility*, p. 112.

19 Aubry, *op. cit.*, p. 267.

20 Helene Deutsch, *The Psychology of Women*, I, pp. 160-61.

21 Healy, *op. cit.*, p. 628; Burt, *op. cit.*, p. 216.

22 Lombroso and Ferrero, *op. cit.*, p. 364.

23 Icard, *op. cit.*, p. 136.

24 Gudden, "Die Zurechnungsfähigkeit bei Warenhausdiebstählen," *Vierteljahrsschrift für Gerichtliche Medizin und Öffentliches Sanitätswesen*, Dritte Folge, XXXIII, Supplementsheft (1907), 66.

25 Kurt Boas, "Forensisch—psychiatrische Kasuistik I," *Archiv für Kriminal-Anthropologie*, XXXV (1909), 227; Lombroso and Ferrero, *op. cit.*, p. 364; Icard, *op. cit.*, pp. 145, 170-72.

26 Gross, *op. cit.*, p. 407; Lombroso and Ferrero, *op. cit.*, p. 364; Buschan, *op. cit.*, p. 11; Hugo Marx, "Ovulation und Schwangerschaft in ihrer Bedeutung für die Forensische Psychiatrie," *Berliner Klinische Wochenschrift*, XLV (1908), 1777; Von Hentig, "Fortpflanzungsphasen und Zurechnungsfähigkeit," *Monatsschrift für Kriminalpsychologie und Strafrechtsreform*, XXI (1930), 155; the same, *Crime: Causes and Conditions*, p. 114.

27 Weinberg, *op. cit.*, pp. 10-15; Healy, *op. cit.*, p. 141-43; Burt, *op. cit.*, p. 368; Deutsch, *Psychology of Women*, I, p. 125.

28 Healy, *op. cit.*, pp. 141-43.

29 Helen Yarnell, "Fire-Setting in Children," *The American Journal of Orthopsychiatry*, X (1940), 273.

30 Georg Ilberg, "Brandstiftung einer Heimwehkranken," *Monatsschrift für Kriminalpsychologie und Strafrechtsreform*, XII (1921-22), 123; A. Werner, "Die Rolle des Schwachsinns in der Kriminalität," *Monatsschrift für Psychiatrie und Neurologie*, CX (1945), 28.

31 Von Hentig, "Fortpflanzungsphasen und Zurechnungsfähigkeit," p. 155.

32 Healy, *op. cit.*, pp. 633-34; Max Fischer, "Schwangerschaft und Diebstahl," *Allgemeine Zeitschrift für Psychiatrie*, LXI (1904), 325; Alexander Pilcz, "Die Verstimmungszustände," *Grenzfragen des Nerven- Und Seelenlebens*, X (1909), Heft 63, p. 22; Hugo Marx, "Ovulation und Schwangerschaft in ihrer Bedeutung für die Forensische Psychiatrie," p. 1778.

33 Healy, *op. cit.*, pp. 634-35; Birnbaum, *Die Psychopathischen Verbrecher*, p. 319; Weinberg, *op. cit.*, p. 25; Von Hentig, "Fortpflanzungsphasen und Zurechnungsfähigkeit," p. 158; Fischer, *op. cit.*, p. 326.

34 Fischer, *op. cit.*, p. 348.

35 Weinberg, *op. cit.*, p. 24.

36 Seward, *op. cit.*, pp. 217 ff.

37 Harry Campbell, *Differences in the Nervous Organisation of Man and Woman*, p. 263; Thomas Watts Eden, *A Manual of Gynecology*, p. 80; Weiss and English, *op. cit.*, p. 255; Curtis, *op. cit.*, p. 95; Edward Allen, "Disturbances of Menstruation" in *A Textbook of Surgery* (Frederick Christopher, Ed.), 2nd rev. ed., p. 1475; Novak, *op. cit.*, p. 133; and many others.

38 Seward, *op. cit.*, p. 219.

39 Deutsch, *Psychoanalyse der weiblichen Sexualfunktionen*, p. 91.

40 Hugo Sellheim, *Gemütsverstimmungen der Frau*, p. 58; Leppmann, *op. cit.*, p. 317; Pilcz, *op. cit.*, p. 22.

41 Von Hentig, *Crime: Causes and Conditions*, p. 115.

42 Von Hentig, *ibid.*

43 Krille, *op. cit.*, p. 15.

44 Leppmann, *op. cit.*, pp. 317-18.

CHAPTER XI

SOCIAL FACTORS IN FEMALE CRIME

Among the environmental factors which have been mentioned as causally related to female crime, emphasis has been placed on the following: (1) differential association, (2) the cultural basis of the desires of women offenders for the results of their criminal behavior, and (3) the accessibility of the object of their criminal attacks.

Differential Association.

As early as 1864, there appeared in England a life history of a professional woman criminal, Jane Cameron, which is an excellent demonstration of the natural history of a criminal career written long before the term was coined.[1] Born of a mother who kept a disorderly house in one of the worst slums of Glasgow and was an alcoholic who neglected her, she grew up without any parental love in her home. At the age of ten she began factory work, and soon received from her "father" the advice that prostitution was an easier means of making a living than drudging along all day in a workroom. She soon turned to the streets, attached herself to a delinquent gang, became friendly with a girl whose parents operated a fence, and finally fell in love with a young thief. Shortly after having fallen in with that gang, she committed her first act of shoplifting, for which she received much acclaim from her friends. Deserted by her mother (the father having disappeared earlier), she went to her girl friend's parents, who advised her to enter the thieving profession. She accepted this advice, received lessons in picking pockets, and became a professional thief.[2]

This short summary of the genesis of a criminal career illustrates perfectly the pattern of family situation and associations which are characteristic of the professional woman offender. The example and the suggestions of criminal parents, the broken home, the character-forming contacts with friends to whom she turned in her attempt to get compensation for the dissatisfactions and final loss of her home, the resolution of possible choices for her to a life of unrewarding drudgery, prostitution, or crime, all are well illustrated in this old and forgotten life history which contains every element that criminological research up to the present has elucidated regarding this aspect of female crime.

The tremendous influence which the criminality of parents or other family members have, not only on the behavior of male, but also of female, offenders is perhaps best corroborated by the fact that the Gluecks found such family situations in the high proportion of 80.7 per cent of their women cases.[3]

Even where the main characteristic of the home is not so much crime as poverty, crowded living conditions and the resulting low standards of sex morality often lead to early sex delinquencies on the part of the girls which slant them for a criminal pattern of life by way of the social conditioning which they receive either in reform schools or in the pursuit of professional or semi-professional prostitution.[4]

Next in the line of causative influences is the broken home, which seems to be significantly correlated with the delinquency of girls by turning them toward other contacts which are often of a criminal nature. The Glueck material revealed that broken homes existed in 58.4 per cent of their cases, and Katherine Du Pre Lumpkin found a proportion of 63.5 per cent of broken homes in her sample of 252 correctional school girls in Wisconsin.[5] As compared with Shideler's estimate of a 25 per cent incidence of broken homes in the family background of the general population,[6] these figures indicate a very impressive preponderance of broken homes in the family background of delinquent girls. Also, a study of delinquent girls in Chicago revealed a relationship to the same effect. It indicated a broken home background for 66.8 per cent of the delinquent girls as against such a background for only 44.8 per cent of nondelinquent girls.[7] For this reason, the adverse influence of broken homes has remained accepted doctrine with regard to delinquent girls, while the respective doctrine with regard to delinquent boys has been largely abandoned. Since in broken homes the missing parent is more frequently the father than the mother, it may be possible that the presence and influence of the former is more necessary for girls than for boys.[8]

But the broken home itself is only the most glaring example of all those situations in which a girl, because of dissatisfaction in her normal setting, turns to substitute situations which afford her criminal associations. Unsatisfactory school situations can have the same effect. Truancy has often been indicated as the start of juvenile delinquency. Girls who are rejected by their schoolmates or are unable to compete successfully at school because of a low I.Q. are apt to turn to the street. Frequently they do not care or do not dare to go home even after school hours. In our modern cities their attempts to pass the time away usually take them downtown. Generally in company with other maladjusted girls, they window-shop, wander around department stores, attend shows, hang around all-night lunch counters, and pretty soon engage in shoplifting and attracting pickups. In this way, they get engaged in petty delinquencies and finally in other types of crime.[9]

In summary, it is either the criminal association in the home or that resulting from the attempts of girls to compensate for the failure of their home or school, which seems to have a decisive influence upon the causation of juvenile delinquency and professional crime. This picture is basically the same for girls and boys. The differential lies only in the role which illicit sex conduct for monetary gain plays in the shaping of the female criminal career, and in the observation that female professional criminals do not specialize in one line as men do. In this respect a somewhat amusing complaint has come from the ranks of the police. According to one police expert, the male crook is a specialist who sticks to his line and thereby facilitates the detection task of the police, once his methods of work have become known; but the female crook is a source of permanent difficulties because she knows no rules, does not specialize, and therefore always poses new riddles to the pestered detectives.[10]

Creation of Criminal Desires.

With respect to the creation of specific desires, the following phenomena have to be considered. In the field of crimes against the person it has been observed that sex repression, envy, jealousy, and vengeance seem to furnish the motives of crime more often for female than for male offenders.[11] The working of our mores furnishes some important clues for an understanding of this observation. Our society, although frowning upon extramarital sex conduct of the members of either sex, shows a certain rigidity with regard to women. Chastity in girls is considered a serious social demand which should be strictly observed. Sex experiences of boys are, if not approved, at least condoned, and sowing wild oats is generally considered as a healthy stage of male development. The virginal bride is an ideal, the groom without sex experience slightly ridiculous and often a serious marital risk. A man is supposed to be faithful to his wife, but if he is not, he finds understanding. A woman is supposed to be faithful to her husband, and if she is not, she is condemned. That such a situation is hard to bear, and must result in a certain amount of compensation or protest, is only logical.

This protest seems to express itself in two significant forms. On the surface of their mental processes, women seem to accept the strict sex morality imposed upon them by our culture and seem to protest against the double standard only by demanding a similarly strict sex morality for men. Psychological tests of sex differentials in ethical judgments have furnished some interesting material in this respect. Male and female students' ratings of the degree of seriousness of various ethical violations showed a marked discrepancy in their judgments on "Intimate Sex Relations Outside Marriage." The men rated such behavior as about equal in seriousness to "Stealing Small Objects from a Store," while the women rated this act next to "Murder" and "Rape."[12] More deeply, however, other satisfactions of the protest desire are being sought by women, and their resulting behavior can frequently lead them into crime.

Unmarried women's subjection to a severe standard of morality seems to lead to vicarious flights into the realm of fantasy, often of a masochistic nature. This masochistic character of the fantasy work of girls and unmarried women has been explained by a biologically based passivity of the female mind.[13] To the sociologist, however, another explanation suggests itself. It seems possible that the social pressures upon the sex behavior of women are so strong that even in their fantasies they are able to realize the satisfaction of their sex urge only by the excuse of being forced into the act. But whether biologically or culturally created, the female desire for substitute satisfaction in the realm of masochistic fantasy has been repeatedly noticed among pubescent girls and hysterics, and thus seems to furnish an explanation of the high incidence of false accusations with sexual content in these offender groups.

Married women, on the other hand, respond to the double standard, not so much by a desire for vicarious experience, as by overt protest. This, however, cannot assert itself in retaliation in kind and finds a substitute in aggressions against the frustrating agent—in other words, the only sex partner which society permits them to have. The solution of the protest situation by aggression against the person who symbolizes the injustive involved in the double standard is often reflected in crimes of passion. In offenses of this character, women do not feel that they commit a crime and—although aware of the violation of the law by their acts—see themselves as the administrators of a higher justice.[14] If the personality of the husband does not make such aggressions practicable, the woman offender turns against some scapegoat in her environment, such as her children or her neighbors. (This revenge desire may furnish the explanation for the observation that the preponderance of married over unmarried women among female offenders seems to be more pronounced in crimes against the person than in crimes against property.) In this respect it is also interesting to note that, according to a comparatively recent study, wives are more emotional than spinsters while there seems to be very little difference between husbands and bachelors.[15] The corresponding evidence in criminal statistics was not sufficient to warrant any conclusion in the purely statistical presentation of the material regarding the influence of the marital factor on female crime. But within the framework of the causational analysis now pursued, the following data may deserve attention.

In the depression year 1933, when economic pressures were undoubtedly very strong, the commitments to state and federal prisons and reformatories in the United States showed the following differential participation of unmarried and married offenders in crimes against property and in crimes against the person.

TABLE 39

FEMALE PRISONERS RECEIVED FROM COURTS IN FEDERAL PRISONS AND
REFORMATORIES, BY MARITAL STATUS, OFFENSE, RACE,
AND NATIVITY, 1933*

Offense	Single	Married	Quotient
Homicide			
Native white	14	46	3.3
Foreign white	..	7	..
Negro	54	83	1.5
Aggravated Assault			
Native white	4	15	3.8
Foreign white	1	2	2.0
Negro	28	44	1.6
Larceny			
Native white	55	85	1.5
Foreign white	6	10	1.7
Negro	61	60	1.0

* Based on U. S. Bureau of the Census, *Prisoners in State and Federal Prisons and Reformatories, 1933*, pp. 35-36.

These figures are interesting in two respects. First of all, they suggest that actually the greater criminal liability of the married among female offenders is more strongly pronounced in the two representative crimes against the person than in the representative crime against property. Second, they show this differential most strongly expressed for native white women and relatively least expressed for negro women. The differential degree of sexual freedom between these two groups thus finds its corroboration in the different strength of the protest factor as a causative agent in crimes against the person committed by married women. The married negro woman with her comparative economic independence and her greater sexual freedom apparently resorts to the protest crimes to a relatively much lesser degree than the differently situated married white woman of native stock. Regarding white women who are foreign born, the figures are too small to permit any meaningful analysis.

German figures corroborate this showing of the American data. Conviction figures reported by Georg von Mayr for the year 1912 show 1,905 unmarried and 24,695 married women convicted of crimes against the person, or a quotient of 5. In crimes against property, the participation of the married women, however, was relatively much weaker, showing 13,317 unmarried women convicted of these offenses as against 18,235 married women, or a quotient of only 1.37.[16] Finally, Belgian statistics for 1900 have been reported to show that of 1,000 women convicted of insults, 769 were married, and of 1,000 convicted of assaults, 706, while the general participation of the married in every thousand female offenders was only 683.[17]

Of course, absolute figures are less instructive than ratios, but it must not be forgotten that interest is here centered on the different liability of the same population regarding two different groups of crimes. The differences in the absolute figures, therefore, cannot be due to differential proportions in the population because it is the same in both instances. Our primary interest is not single women versus married women as criminals, but rather these two groups and their criminal liability with reference to specific offense categories.

Next to the double standard in our sex morality, it is the exploitation of a specifically female role by modern sales techniques which deserves attention as a desire-promoting factor that may lead women into crime. In the organization of the modern department store and food market with self-service, everything is directed at increasing the temptation for women to buy more than they intend. Woman the shopper is trapped to buy when she enters such a store. If she has weak inhibitions or is pathological, she is almost trapped to steal. Appealing to her desire to fulfill her function as a shopper as efficiently as possible, sales advertisements and catalogues invite her to visit. In the department stores particularly, everything is planned, not only to get her into the store, but also to keep her there and by so doing to expose her to the magic circle of temptation for the longest possible time. If a woman shopper is tired, she need not end her visit.

The department store has restaurants and rest rooms at her disposal so that she can recover her strength. Dubuisson reported that some women considered the department stores in Paris practically as their second home and sometimes visited them as a part of their daily routine.[18] Thus, the desire for efficiency in shopping is exploited by modern sales techniques to such a degree that women often overstep the bounds of reason in their purchases. The seeming opportunity to shop efficiently has become in many instances a temptation to buy more than is needed or more than the budget of the shopper justifies. Irrationality is actually fostered in the creation of desires in the female shopper. The artificial environment of the department stores organized to arouse such desires has also provoked a great amount of crime. And it was just the irrationality of shoplifting which has aroused attention.[19] The quantitative consequences of this phenomenon for the sum total of female crime which have been discussed in Chapter V must be recalled in order to assess the importance of this social factor for the criminality of women.

Finally, female pursuit of domestic service produces a situation of social inferiority and culture conflict in our society which also creates desires causing a great volume of female crime. Large numbers of women who go into domestic service come from the country to the city and are thus faced with the conflict between rural and urban culture.[20] In Europe they are often adolescent and in the United States they are largely members of other races or ethnic stocks than their employers. If they are live-in maids, their living arrangements are often far below the quality of those of their employers.[21] Even if they come in only during the daytime, they are surrounded by a degree of comfort and a standard of living which are in great contrast to their own homes. In either case the daily observance of the better living conditions which their employers enjoy must often lead to envy and resentment which, in their turn, may lead to criminal behavior. There is hardly any other occupation where the experience of differences in the living standards of employer and employee is so much part of the daily job content as in the case of domestics, and the psychological reactions to such a situation can be hardly an object of doubt. This situation is aggravated by the fact that the personal relationship between employer and employee which in earlier times mitigated antagonisms by a feeling of loyalty has been replaced by a purely financial and basically short-time arrangement. The employer's feeling of personal obligation toward the servant has disappeared, and the retainer has been replaced by an antagonistic wage earner.[22]

In the United States, this economic antagonism is further aggravated by race conflict due to the large number of colored women among the domestics. This type of occupation proves to the colored woman, first of all, that she has been forced into a low-wage and low-status group.[23] Furthermore, her very journey to the working place demonstrates to the colored domestic her social inferiority by forcing her to make the daily change from her own poor residential section to the restricted zone of white residences.

Thus, the whole situation of female domestic service, whether white or colored, breeds feelings of frustration and creates a desire for revenge; and this desire can be satisfied very easily due to the particular opportunities offered by this occupation, as will become apparent in the discussion below.

Accessibility of the Objects of Criminal Attack.

There remains the task of investigating to what degree social conditions increase the accessibility of the objects of criminal attack to the woman offender. Again, it is the nature of their social roles which provides women with special opportunities in this respect.

Statistical analysis has already indicated that married women have a higher criminal liability than the unmarried and that this expresses itself particularly in crimes against the person. It has been said that this is so because the unmarried have fewer close relations to a distinct circle of persons than the married.[24] It is undoubtedly true that marriage adds a husband and very often children to the possible personal objects of a woman's criminal attacks. Furthermore, the married woman in her traditional role of housewife has more opportunities to engage in conflict with her neighbors than the single woman, who in our society is usually at work and under the restraining influence of an employment relationship. It is the comparative leisure of the housewife which creates opportunities for friction that do not exist for the working woman, and swells the incidence of petty offenses committed by women.

In crimes against property, particularly the opportunities for stealing seem to be relatively greater for a woman than for a man. The articles which the department stores and food markets offer for purchase are made extremely accessible to her. The shopper is not only permitted to see but also to touch and to try the sales objects. No individual sales effort of a store employee keeps her under obvious control before she has expressed her desire to buy. Household employment equally offers many such easy opportunities. Objects which incite a domestic's desire are handled by her daily as a part of her job, and frequently in the absence of her employer.

With regard to sex delinquency and sex offenses of women in general, our cultural pattern of behavior assists the woman offender by making it unnecessary for her to seek the opportunity. It is actually brought to her by the traditional behavior of man. In our society, man has to take the active part in establishing a personal relationship with woman. The girl who is a sex delinquent has to do little more than to accept the offers tendered to her by men. In addition to this general situation, there are certain female occupations especially conducive to sex immorality because of their implication of social inferiority in comparison with the man who proposes the offense. The occupation of the female domestic, and particularly of the colored female servant in the South, contains special perils in this respect.[25] In addition to the implication of sexual compliance with a male of higher class or caste, there also may be readiness on her part to seek compensatory satisfaction in this type of delinquency. A sexual relationship with her employer may just as well be a revenge on the mistress of the household as a yielding to the status of the husband. Finally, the removal from her home environment, with its loss of primary group control, may permit a domestic to find compensation for the unpleasantness of her job in sex delinquency in her free time.[26]

To sum up, conditioning for a criminal career seems to be as effective with females as it is with males, the only difference being that women have special opportunities to include prostitution within such a career. In addition to the professional criminals socially created, we have found that our society induces special desires in women which can easily lead them into criminal behavior. Finally, our society offers special opportunities, not equally open to men, for satisfying such desires. If we consider that these crime-promoting factors influence a population group which is characterized by psychologically disturbing biological crises, one can but marvel at the masked character of female crime, which can so conceal the results as to give the impression that women are less criminal than men.

NOTES

[1] F. W. Robinson, *Memoirs of Jane Cameron, Female Convict.*

[2] Robinson, *op. cit.,* I, pp. 1-81.

[3] Sheldon and Eleanor T. Glueck, *op. cit.,* p. 72.

[4] Breckinridge and Abbott, *op. cit.,* pp. 106-7; Richmond, *op. cit.,* pp. 118-19; Gillin, *op. cit.,* p. 173; Bishop, *From Information Received,* p. 36; Burt, *op. cit.,* p. 85.

[5] Sheldon and Eleanor T. Glueck, *op. cit.,* pp. 70-71; Katherine Du Pre Lumpkin, "Factors in the Commitment of Correctional School Girls in Wisconsin," *The American Journal of Sociology,* XXXVII (1931-32), 225.

[6] Ernest H. Shideler, "Family Disintegration and the Delinquent Boy in the United States," *Journal of the American Institute of Criminal Law and Criminology,* VIII (1917-18), 718.

[7] Sutherland, *op. cit.,* 3rd ed., p. 159. (Referring to Margaret Hodgkiss, "The Influence of Broken Homes and Working Mothers," *Smith College Studies in Social Work,* 3:259-274, March 1933.)

[8] Sutherland, *op. cit.,* 3rd ed., p. 159.

[9] Mary Louise Webb, "Delinquency in the Making," *Journal of Social Hygiene,* XXIX (1943), 508-9.

[10] Bishop, *Women and Crime,* p. 5.

[11] Puibaraud, *op. cit.,* p. 415; Aubry, *op. cit.,* p. 271.

[12] E. B. Skaggs, "Sex Differences in Moral Attitudes," *The Journal of Social Psychology,* XI (1940), 6-7.

[13] Deutsch, *The Psychology of Women,* I, pp. 251, 255-56.

[14] Hugo Marx, "Schuld und Strafe," *Archiv für Kriminal-Anthropologie,* XLII (1911), 347-48; Puibaraud, *op. cit.,* p. 414.

[15] Raymond Royce Willoughby, "The Relationship to Emotionality of Age, Sex and Conjugal Condition," *The American Journal of Sociology,* XLIII (1937-38), 922-23.

[16] Based on Von Mayr, *op. cit.,* p. 803.

[17] Jacquart, *op. cit.,* p. 82.

[18] Dubuisson, *op. cit.,* pp. 341-43.

[19] Lombroso and Ferrero, *op. cit.,* p. 459; Dubuisson, *op. cit.,* p. 4; Wilhelm Stekel, "The Sexual Root of Kleptomania," *The Journal of the American In-*

stitute of Criminal Law and Criminology, II (1911-12), 239; McNally, *op. cit.*, p. 57; Antheaume, *op. cit.*, pp. 26-48.

[20] Lombroso and Ferrero, *op. cit.*, p. 460.

[21] De Ryckère, *La Criminalité Ancillaire*, pp. 511, 536.

[22] Corre, *op. cit.*, pp. 516-17.

[23] Myrdal, *op. cit.*, II, p. 1085.

[24] Schmitz, *op. cit.*, p. 11; Aschaffenburg, *op. cit.*, p. 166.

[25] Sutherland, *op. cit.*, 2nd ed., p. 160; John Dollard, *Caste and Class in a Southern Town*, p. 147.

[26] W. I. Thomas, *The Unadjusted Girl*, p. 118.

Girls based on Intensive Studies of 500 Cases," *Journal of Criminal Law and Criminology*, XIII (1922-23), 494-586.

Birnbaum, Karl. *Die Psychopathischen Verbrecher*. Berlin: P. Langenscheidt, 1914. Pp. 568.

————. "Die sexuellen Falschbeschuldigungen der Hysterischen," *Archiv für Kriminal-Anthropologie*, LXIV (1915), 1-39.

Bishop, Cecil. *Women and Crime*. London: Chatto and Windus, 1931. Pp. 295.

————. *From Information Received*. London: Hutchinson and Co., Ltd., 1932. Pp. 286.

Bleuler, Eugen. *Textbook of Psychiatry*, authorized English ed. by A. A. Brill. New York: The Macmillan Company, 1924. Pp. xviii + 635.

Bloch, Iwan, and Loewenstein, George. *Die Prostitution*, II, 1. Berlin: Louis Marcus Verlagsbuchhandlung, 1925. Pp. viii + 728.

Boas, Kurt. "Forensisch-psychiatrische Kasuistik I," *Archiv für Kriminal-Anthropologie*, XXXV (1909), 195-248.

Bodio, L. "Rapport sur la méthode du bulletin individuel appliquée à la statistique judiciaire pénale en Italie depuis l'année 1890," *Bulletin de l'Institut International de Statistique*, XII (1900), 371-77.

Böhmer, K. "Kriminelle Thalliumvergiftung," *Deutsche Zeitschrift für die Gesamte Gerichtliche Medizin*, XXX (1938), 146-50.

Bonger, William A. *Criminality and Economic Conditions*. Boston: Little, Brown, and Company, 1916. Pp. xxxii + 706.

————. *Race and Crime*. New York: Columbia University Press, 1943. Pp. x + 130.

Bonos, Arlene Helen. "Roumany Rye of Philadelphia," *American Anthropologist*, N. S., XLIV (1942), 257-74.

Boos, William F. *The Poison Trail*. Boston: Hale, Cushman & Flint, 1939. Pp. 380.

Bossard, James H. S. "War and the Family," *American Sociological Review*, VI (1941), 330-44.

Bowman, Mary Jean. "Economic Aspects of the Histories of Reformatory Women" (A Study of Women Committed to the Massachusetts State Reformatory from July 1, 1931 to July 1, 1933). Radcliffe College, 1938, unpublished. Pp. 460.

Breckinridge, Sophonisba Preston, and Abbott, Edith. *The Delinquent Child and the Home*. New York Charities Publication Committee, 1912. Pp. x + 355.

Bresler, Johannes. "Die pathologische Anschuldigung," *Juristisch-psychiatrische Grenzfragen*, V, No. 8 (1907), pp. 1-42.

Bronner, Augusta F. *A Comparative Study of the Intelligence of Delinquent Girls*. New York City: Teachers College, Columbia University, Contributions to Education, No. 68, 1914. Pp. 95.

Brouardel, P. *L'infanticide*. Paris: J. B. Baillière, 1897. Pp. viii + 402.

Bryan, Albert W. "Arsenic Poisoning. Case report of arsenical poisoning with homicidal intent," *The Wisconsin Medical Journal*, XXXVIII (1939), 545-48.

Burch, Lucius E. "Treatment of Abortion," *Journal of the Tennessee State Medical Association*, XXI (1928-29), 172-75.

Burchardt, Hans Hermann. *Kriminalität in Stadt und Land*. Abhandlungen des Kriminalistischen Institutes an der Universität Berlin. Berlin and Leipzig: Walter de Gruyter & Co., 1936. Pp. 168.

Burleigh, Edith N., and Harris, Frances R. *The Delinquent Girl*. New York: The New York School of Social Work, Studies in Social Work, Child Welfare Series, Monograph No. 3, 1923. Pp. 118.

Burt, Cyril Lodowic. *The Young Delinquent*. New York: D. Appleton and Company, 1925. Pp. xvi + 619.

Buschan, Georg. *Geschlecht und Verbrechen*. Berlin and Leipzig: Hermann Seemann Nachfolger; 3rd ed., n. d. Pp. 96.

Byrnes, Thomas (Inspector Byrnes). *Professional Criminals of America*. New York: Cassell and Company, 1886. Pp. 433.

Campbell, Harry. *Differences in the Nervous Organisation of Man and Woman*. London: H. K. Lewis, 1891. Pp. xii + 383.

Carstens, C. C. "Neglected Children," in "Child," *Encyclopaedia of the Social Sciences*, III (New York: The Macmillan Company, 1930), 403-6.

Cassity, J. H. "Sociopsychiatric Aspects of Female Felons," *The Journal of Criminal Psychopathology*, III (1941-42), 597-604.

Chadwick, Mary. *The Psychological Effects of Menstruation*. New York: Nervous and Mental Disease Publishing Company, 1932. Pp. 70.

Charity Organization Society of the City of New York, The Committee on Criminal Courts of the. *The Adolescent Offender*. New York: 1923. Pp. 85.

Chesterton, Mrs. Cecil. *Women of the Underworld*. London: Stanley Paul & Co., Ltd., 1928. Pp. 255.

Christison, J. Sanderson, M.D. *Crime and Criminals*. Chicago: The W. T. Keener Company, 1897. Pp. 117.

City Council Committee on Crime of the City of Chicago, Report of. Chicago: 1915. Pp. vi + 196.

Colajanni, Napoleone. *Sociologia Criminale*, II. Catania: F. Tropea, 1889. Pp. viii + 704.

Conyngton, Mary. "Relation between Occupation and Criminality of Women," in *Report on Conditions of Woman and Child Wage Earners in the United States*, XV (1911). 61st Congress, 2nd Session, Senate Document No. 645. Pp. 119.

Corre, Armand. *Crime et Suicide*. Paris: Octave Doin, 1891. Pp. vi + 654.

Costello, Marie E. "Some Indications of Trend in Female Criminality in the United States." Unpublished paper.

Cummin, William. *The Proofs of Infanticide.* London, 1836. Pp. viii + 95.

Curran, Frank J. "Specific Trends in Criminality of Women," *Journal of Criminal Psychopathology*, III (1941-42), 605-24.

Curtis, Arthur Hale. *A Textbook of Gynecology.* Philadelphia: W. B. Saunders Publishing Co.; 5th ed., 1946. Pp. xvi + 755.

Darrow, Clarence. *Crime, Its Causes and Treatment.* New York: Thomas Y. Crowell Company, 1922. Pp. x + 292.

Deutsch, Helene. *Psychoanalyse der weiblichen Sexualfunktionen.* Leipzig: Internationaler Psychoanalytischer Verlag, 1925. Pp. 111.

———. *The Psychology of Women*, I. New York: Grune and Stratton, 1944, Pp. xiv + 399.

Devon, James. *The Criminal and the Community.* New York: John Lane Company, 1912. Pp. xxii + 348.

Dilnot, George. *The Story of Scotland Yard.* Boston: Houghton Mifflin Company, 1927. Pp. x + 340.

Dollard, John. *Caste and Class in a Southern Town.* New Haven: Yale University Press, 1937. Pp. viii + 502.

Dubuisson, Paul. "Les Voleuses des Grands Magasins," *Archives d'Anthropologie Criminelle*, XVI (1901), 1-20, 341-70.

Eden, Thomas Watts. *A Manual of Gynecology.* London: J. and A. Churchill, 1911. Pp. xxii + 632.

Ellington, George. *The Women of New York.* New York: The New York Book Company, 1869. Pp. 650.

Elo, Oiva. "Der Kindesmord in der Kriminalstatistik," *Deutsche Zeitschrift für die Gesamte Gerichtliche Medizin*, XXXII (1939-40), 1-47.

Exner, Franz. *Krieg und Kriminalität in Österreich.* Wien: Hölder-Pichler-Tempsky A. G.; New Haven: Yale University Press, 1927. Pp. xiv + 217 and 24 (Anhang).

———. "Die Reichskriminalstatistik 1935-1938," *Monatsschrift für Kriminalbiologie und Strafrechtsreform*, XXXIII (1942), 102-10.

Farley, Phil. *Criminals of America.* New York; author's ed., 1876. Pp. xvi + 638.

Fernald, Mabel Ruth, *et al. A Study of Women Delinquents in New York State.* New York: The Century Company, 1920. Pp. xviii + 542.

Ferrero, Guglielmo. "Le Mensonge et la Véracité chez la Femme Criminelle," *Archives D'Anthropologie Criminelle*, VIII (1893), 138-50.

Finot, Jean. *Préjugé et Probleme des Sexes.* Paris: Félix Alcan, 1912. Pp. 524.

Fischer, Max. "Schwangerschaft und Diebstahl," *Allgemeine Zeitschrift für Psychiatrie*, LXI (1904), 312-54.

Fletcher, Joseph A. "Shoplifting Can Be Licked," *Chainstore Age* (Grocery Executive ed.), December 1940, pp. 30, 50-54.

Gillin, John Lewis. *Criminology and Penology.* New York: D. Appleton-Century Company; 3rd ed., 1945. Pp. xii + 615.

Glueck, Sheldon and Eleanor T. *Five Hundred Delinquent Women*. New York: Alfred A. Knopf, 1934. Pp. xxiv + 539 + x.

Goodwin, John C. *Sidelights on Criminal Matters*. New York: George H. Doran Company, 1923. Pp. 336.

Göring, M. H. "Kriminalpsychologie," in *Handbuch der Vergleichenden Psychologie*, III, Abteilung 2, n. d., pp. 155-229.

Granier, C. *La Femme Criminelle*. Paris: Octave Doin, 1906. Pp. x + 468.

Greeff, Etienne De. *Introduction à la Criminologie*. Louvain; Editions de L'Ecrou, 1937. Pp. iv + 362.

Griffiths, Arthur. "Female Criminals," *The North American Review*, CLXI (1895), 141-52.

Gross, Hans. *Kriminalpsychologie*. Leipzig: F. C. W. Vogel; 2nd ed., 1905. Pp. xii + 701.

Growdon, Clarence H. "The Mental Status of Reformatory Women," *Journal of the American Institute of Criminal Law and Criminology*, XXII (1931-32), 196-220.

Gudden (no first name indicated). "Die Zurechnungsfähigkeit bei Warenhausdiebstahlen," *Vierteljahrsschrift für Gerichtliche Medizin und Öffentliches Sanitätswesen*, Dritte Folge, XXXIII, Supplementheft (1907), 64-69.

Guibord, Alberta S. B. "Physical States of Criminal Women," *Journal of the American Institute of Criminal Law and Criminology*, VIII (1917-18), 82-95.

Guild, Arthur Alden. *Baby Farms in Chicago*. An Investigation made for the Juvenile Protective Association. Chicago, 1917. Pp. 27.

Haberda, Albin. "Zur Lehre vom Kindesmorde," *Beiträge zur Gerichtlichen Medizin*, I (Leipzig, 1911), 38-191.

Hacker, E. "Internationale Kriminalstatistik," *Monatsschrift für Kriminalpsychologie und Strafrechtsreform*, XXII (1931), 269-79.

———. "Soziale Kapillarität und Kriminalität," *Monatsschrift für Kriminalbiologie und Strafrechtsreform*, XXVIII (1937), 353-64.

———. *Die Kriminalität des Kantons Zürich*. Miskolc; author's ed., 1939. Pp. xvi + 311.

Hall, Gladys Mary. *Prostitution in the Modern World*. New York: Emerson Books, Inc., 1936. Pp. 200.

Hamilton, Allan McLane, and Godkin, Lawrence. *A System of Legal Medicine*, II. New York: E. B. Treat, 1894. Pp. 738.

Handman, Max Sylvius. "Abortion," in *Encyclopaedia of the Social Sciences*, I (New York: The Macmillan Company, 1930), 372-74.

Harding, M. Esther. *The Way of All Women*. London: Longmans, Green and Co., 1935. Pp. xvi + 335.

Harnack, Erich. *Die gerichtliche Medizin*. Leipzig: Akademische Verlagsgesellschaft, m.b.H., 1914. Pp. xiv + 448.

Haynes, Fred E. *Criminology*. New York: McGraw-Hill Book Company, Inc.; 2nd ed., 1935. Pp. xii + 497.

Healy, William. *The Individual Delinquent*. Boston: Little, Brown, and Company, 1915. Pp. xvi + 830.

Healy, William, and Healy, Mary Tenney. *Pathological Lying, Accusation, and Swindling, A Study in Forensic Psychology*. Criminal Science Monographs No. 1. Boston: Little, Brown, and Company, 1915. Pp. x + 286.

Heindl, Robert. "Das Weib als Mörderin," *Archiv für Kriminologie*, XCV (1934), 61-63.

Henderson, D. K., and Gillespie, R. D. *A Text-Book of Psychiatry for Students and Practitioners*. New York: Oxford University Press; 5th ed., 1941. Pp. xii + 660.

Hentig, Hans von. "Fortpflanzungsphasen und Zurechnungsfähigkeit," *Monatsschrift für Kriminalpsychologie und Strafrechtsreform*, XXI (1930), 149-60.

——. *Crime: Causes and Conditions*. New York: McGraw-Hill Book Company, Inc., 1947. Pp. xiv + 379.

——. "The Criminality of the Colored Woman," *University of Colorado Studies*, Series C, I, No. 3 (1942), pp. 231-60.

Herx, Liselotte. *Der Giftmord, inbesondere der Giftmord durch Frauen, Eine Untersuchung auf sociologisch-biologisch-psychologischer Grundlage*. Emsdetten: Verlagsanstalt Heinr. & J. Lechte, 1937. Pp. 202.

Herz, Hugo. "Die Kriminalität des Weibes nach den Ergebnissen der neueren österreichischen Statistik," *Archiv für Kriminal-Anthropologie*, XVIII (1905), 285-303.

Hey, Emil. "Die Vitriolseuche in Russland," *Archiv für Kriminal-Anthropologie*, LVII (1914), 311-15.

Hippocrates. *Oeuvres Complètes*, trans. into French by E. Littré. Paris: J. B. Baillière, 1846. V, pp. 735; VIII, pp. 676.

Hirning, L. Clovis. "Indecent Exposure and Other Sex Offenses," *Journal of Clinical Psychopathology*, VII (1945-46), pp. 105-14.

Hoegel, Hugo. "Die Straffalligkeit des Weibes," *Archiv für Kriminal-Anthropologie*, V (1900), 231-89.

Hollingworth, Leta Stetter. *Functional Periodicity*. New York: Teachers College, Columbia University, 1914. Pp. viii + 101.

Hoover, J. Edgar. "The Women in Crime," *This Week*, magazine section of the *Detroit News*, October 17, 1937.

Hübner (no first name indicated). "Kriminalpsychologisches über das weibliche Geschlecht," *Allgemeine Zeitschrift für Psychiatrie*, LXIX (1912), 276-79.

Hudig, Johanna C. *De Criminaliteit Der Vrouw*. Utrecht: Dekker & Van De Vegt, n. v., 1940. Pp. xii + 258.

Hurwicz, E. "Kriminalität und Prostitution der weiblichen Dienstboten," *Archiv für Kriminal-Anthropologie*, LXV (1916), 185-251.

Hutchinson, William. *A Dissertation on Infanticide in its Relations to Physiology and Jurisprudence.* London: 1820. Pp. 99.

Icard, S. *La Femme pendant la Période Menstruelle.* Paris: Félix Alcan, 1890. Pp. xiv + 283.

Ilberg, Georg. "Brandstiftung einer Heimwehkranken," *Monatsschrift für Kriminalpsychologie und Strafrechtsreform,* XII (1921-22), 117-26.

Irving, H. B. *A Book of Remarkable Criminals.* London: Cassell and Company, Ltd., 1918. Pp. viii + 336.

Jacquart, Camille. *La Criminalité Belge, 1868-1909.* Louvain: Institut Supérieur de Philosophie, 1912. Pp. 140.

Jassny, Alexander. "Zur Psychologie der Verbrecherin," *Archiv für Kriminal-Anthropologie,* XLII (1911), 90-107.

Jerome, Helen. *The Secret of Woman.* London: Chapman & Hall, Ltd., 1923. Pp. 240.

Kellor, Frances A. "Criminal Sociology—Criminality Among Women," *Arena,* XXIII (1900), 516-24.

———. "Psychological and Environmental Study of Women Criminals," *The American Journal of Sociology,* V (1900), 527-43, 671-82.

———. "The Criminal Negro," *Arena,* XXV (1901), 58-68, 190-97, 308-16, 419-28, 510-20.

———. *Experimental Sociology.* New York: The Macmillan Company, 1901. Pp. xvi + 316.

Kinsey, Alfred C.; Pomeroy, Wardell B.; and Martin, Clyde E. *Sexual Behavior in the Human Male.* Philadelphia: W. B. Saunders Company, 1948. Pp. xvi + 804.

Kopp, Marie E. *Birth Control in Practice.* New York: Robert M. McBride & Company, 1934. Pp. xxvi + 31-290.

Koppenfels, Sebastian von. *Die Kriminalität der Frau im Kriege.* Leipzig: Ernst Wiegandt, 1926. Pp. 59.

Krafft-Ebing, Richard von. *Psychosis Menstrualis.* Stuttgart: Ferdinand Enke Verlag, 1902. Pp. 112.

Krille, Hans. *Weibliche Kriminalität und Ehe.* Leipzig: Ernst Wiegandt, 1931. Pp. 64.

Lacassagne, A. "Notes statistiques sur l'empoisonnement criminel en France," *Archives D'Anthropologie Criminelle,* I (1886), 260-64.

———. *Peine de Mort et Criminalité.* Paris: A. Maloine, 1908. Pp. 184.

Leale, Dr. H. "De la Criminalité des Sexes," *Archives D'Anthropologie Criminelle,* XXV (1910), 401-30.

Lekkerkerker, Eugenia C. *Reformatories for Women in the United States.* The Hague: J. B. Wolters' Uitgevers-Maatschappij, n.v., 1931. Pp. xvi + 615.

Leppmann, Friedrich. "Weibliche Generationsphasen und Kriminalität," *Archiv für Frauenkunde und Konstitutionsforschung,* XIV (1928), 292-321.

Liepmann, Moritz. *Krieg und Kriminalität in Deutschland.* Stuttgart,

Berlin, and Leipzig: Deutsche Verlagsanstalt; New Haven: Yale University Press, 1930. Pp. xiv + 197.

Lipmann, Otto. "Zur Beurteilung von Aussagen junger Mädchen," *Archiv für Kriminal-Anthropologie*, LXXIX (1926), 53-57.

Locard, Edmond. *Le Crime et les Criminels*. Paris: La Renaissance du Livre, n.d. Pp. 278.

Lombroso, Cesare. *Crime: Its Causes and Remedies*. Boston: Little, Brown, and Company, 1911. Pp. xlvi + 471.

——, and Ferrero, Guglielmo. *Das Weib als Verbrecherin und Prostituierte*, trans. by H. Kurella. Hamburg: Verlagsanstalt & Druckerei A. G., 1894. Pp. xvi + 590.

Lombroso Ferrero, Gina. *Criminal Man*. New York and London: G. P. Putnam's Sons, 1911. Pp. xx + 322.

——. "I Delitti Femminili e le Nuove Professioni della Donna," *Archivio di Antropologia Criminale*, L (1930), 839-42. [Psychological Abstracts, V (1931), No. 2801.]

Lönne (no first name indicated). "Über die Zunahme der Fruchtabtreibungen vom Standpunkt der Volksgesundheit und Rassenhygiene," Kleinere Mitteilungen, *Archiv für Kriminologie*, LXXX (1927), 59-62.

Loosjes, Cornelis. *Bijdrage Tot De Studie Van De Criminaliteit Der Vrouw*. Harlem: De Erven Loosjes, 1894. Pp. xvi + 244.

Lop, P. A. "Les Attentats à la Pudeur des Femmes sur des Petits Garçons," *Archives d'Anthropologie Criminelle*, X (1895), 37-42.

Low, Frances H. "A Remedy for Babyfarming," *The Fortnightly Review*, LXIII, N. S. (1898), 280-86.

Lucas, Netley. *Crook Janes*, A Study of the Woman Criminal the World Over. London: Stanley Paul & Company, Ltd., 1926. Pp. 236.

Lumpkin, Katharine Du Pre. "Factors in the Commitment of Correctional School Girls in Wisconsin," *The American Journal of Sociology*, XXXVII (1931-32), 222-30.

Lunden, Walter A. *Statistics on Crime and Criminals*. Pittsburgh: Stevenson and Foster Company, 1942. Pp. xviii + 263.

McNally, William D., M.D. *Medical Jurisprudence and Toxicology*. Philadelphia: W. B. Saunders Company, 1939. Pp. 386.

Maine Medical Association—Committee on Maternal and Child Welfare. "Abortion," *The Journal of the Maine Medical Association*, XXXIV (1943), 72-74.

Marx, Hugo. "Ovulation und Schwangerschaft in ihrer Bedeutung für die Forensische Psychiatrie," *Berliner Klinische Wochenschrift*, XLV (1908), 1776-78.

——. "Schuld und Strafe," *Archiv für Kriminal-Anthropologie*, XLII (1911), 304-51; XLIII (1911), 91-118.

Mathews, Ellen. "A Study of Emotional Stability in Children," *The Journal of Delinquency*, VIII (1923), 1-40.

Mathews, Julia. "A Survey of 341 Delinquent Girls in California," *The Journal of Delinquency*, VIII (1923), 196-231.

Mayr, Georg von. *Statistik und Gesellschaftslehre*, III. Tübingen: Mohr, 1917. Pp. viii + 1042.

Mazer, Charles, and Israel, S. Leon. *Diagnosis and Treatment of Menstrual Disorders and Sterility*. New York: Paul B. Hoeber, Inc., 1941. Pp. x + 485.

Melegari, Dora. "La Femme Criminelle en Italie," *Le Correspondant*, CCX (1903), 524-49.

Mendenhall, Georgiana S. "A Study of Behavior Problems," *The Psychological Clinic*, XXI (1932-33), 77-113.

Mercier, Charles. *Crime and Criminals*. New York: Henry Holt and Company, 1919. Pp. xviii + 290.

Meredith, Susanna. "Some Peculiarities of Criminals," *Proceedings of the Annual Congress of the National Prison Association of the United States, Held at Nashville, Nov. 16-20, 1889* (Chicago, 1890), pp. 222-32.

Miller, Justin. *Handbook of Criminal Law*. St. Paul: West Publishing Co., 1934. Pp. xiv + 649.

Minovici, M. "Remarques Sur La Criminalité Féminine en Roumanie," *Archives d'Anthropologie Criminelle*, XXII (1907), 565-79.

Mitchell, C. Ainsworth. *Science and the Criminal*. Boston: Little, Brown, and Company, 1911. Pp. xiv + 240.

Mönkemöller (no first name indicated). "Sittlichkeitsdelikt und Psychologie der Aussage," *Archiv für Kriminal-Anthropologie*, LXXVIII (1926), 126-72, 248-57.

Mönkemöller, Otto. *Korrektionsanstalt und Landarmenhaus, Ein soziologischer Beitrag zur Kriminalität und Psychopathologie des Weibes*. Leipzig: J. A. Barth, 1908. Pp. vi + 240.

Morrison, William Douglas. *Crime and its Causes*. London: S. Sonnenschein and Company, 1891. Pp. x + 236.

Morton, J. H. "Female Homicides," *The Journal of Mental Science*, LXXX (1934), 64-74.

Myrdal, Gunnar. *An American Dilemma*, II. New York: Harper and Brothers, 1944. Pp. xiv + 709-1483.

National Committee on Maternal Health, Inc. *The Abortion Problem*. Baltimore: The Williams & Wilkins Company, 1944. Pp. xii + 182.

New York City, Mayor's Committee for the Study of Sex Offenses. Report. New York: n. d. Pp. 100.

Niceforo, Alfredo. *Criminologia ** Ambiente e Delinquenza*. Milano: Fratelli Bocca-Editori, 1943. Pp. viii + 739.

Novak, Emil. *Menstruation and Its Disorders*. New York: D. Appleton and Company, 1921. Pp. xviii + 357.

Parmelee, Maurice. *Criminology*. New York: The Macmillan Company, 1918. Pp. xiv + 522.

Parr, Robert J. *The Baby Farmer*. London: National Society for the Prevention of Cruelty to Children, 2nd ed., 1909. Pp. 77.

Pearson, Edmund. *Murder at Smutty Nose and other Murders*. Boston: Doubleday, Page & Company, 1926. Pp. x + 330.

Pike, Luke Owen. *A History of Crime in England*, II. London: Smith, Elder & Co., 1876. Pp. xx + 719.

Pilcz, Alexander. "Die Verstimmungszustände," *Grenzfragen des Nerven und Seelenlebens*, X (1909), Heft 63. Pp. 43.

Pinkham, Charles B., M.D. "The Pacific Coast Abortion Ring," *Federation Bulletin*, XXIII (1937), 36-54.

Pollitz, Paul. *Die Psychologie des Verbrechers*. Berlin and Leipzig: B. G. Teubner, 1925. Pp. 128.

Prinzing, Fr. "Der Einfluss der Ehe auf die Kriminalität des Mannes," *Zeitschrift für Sozialwissenschaft*, II Alte Folge (1899), 37-44.

——. "Die Erhöhung der Kriminalität des Weibes durch die Ehe," *Zeitschrift für Sozialwissenschaft*, II Alte Folge (1899), 433-50.

——. "Soziale Faktoren der Kriminalität," *Zeitschrift für die gesamte Strafrechtswissenschaft*, XXII (1902), 551-88.

Proal, Louis. *Le Crime et La Peine*. Paris: Félix Alcan, 1892. Pp. xvi + 544.

Puibaraud, Louis. "La femme criminelle," *Grande Revue*, XII (April-June 1899), 393-427.

Puppe, G. "Zur Psychologie und Prophylaxe des Kindesmordes," *Deutsche Medizinische Wochenschrift*, XLIII (1917), 609-13.

Quirós, C. Bernaldo de, and Aguilaniedo, J. M. L. *Verbrechertum und Prostitution in Madrid*. Berlin: L. Marcus, 1910. Pp. xx + 317.

Radzinowicz, L. "Variability of the Sex-Ratio of Criminality," *The Sociological Review*, XXIX (1937), 76-102.

Raimann, Emil. "Über Warenhausdiebinnen," *Monatsschrift für Kriminalpsychologie und Strafrechtsreform*, XIII (1922), 300-21.

Reckless, Walter C. *Criminal Behavior*. New York: McGraw-Hill Book Company, 1940. Pp. xii + 532.

——. *The Etiology of Delinquent and Criminal Behavior*. New York: Social Science Research Council, 1943. Pp. xii + 169.

Richmond, Winifred. *The Adolescent Girl*. New York: The Macmillan Company, 1926. Pp. xvi + 212.

Robinson, F. W. *Memoirs of Jane Cameron, female convict*. London: Hurst & Blackett, 1864. I, pp. 326; II, pp. 301.

Roesner, Ernst. "Die internationale Kriminalstatistik in ihrer methodischen Entwicklung," *Allgemeines Statistiches Archiv*, XXII (1932), 17-44.

——. "Alter und Straffälligkeit," *Handwörterbuch der Kriminologie* (Alexander Elster and Heinrich Lingemann, eds.), Berlin: Walter de Gruyter & Co., 1933. I, pp. 22-35.

Roesner, Ernst. "Familienstand," *Handwörterbuch der Kriminologie,* I, pp. 398-414.

——. "Zur Frage der weiblichen Kriminalität," discussed in *Monatsschrift für Kriminalbiologie und Strafrechtsreform,* XXVIII (1937), Sprechsaal, p. 484-85.

Roncoroni, L. "Influenza del Sesso sulla criminalità in Italia," *Archivio di Psichiatria, Science Penali et Antropologia Criminale,* XIV (1893), 1-14.

Rongy, A. J. *Abortion: Legal or Illegal?* New York: The Vanguard Press, 1933. Pp. 212.

Runnels, Scott C. "Criminal Abortion as a Public Health Problem," *The Journal of the American Institute of Homeopathy,* XXXIII (1940), 491-93.

Ryckère, Raymond de. *La femme en prison et devant le mort, Etude de Criminologie.* Lyon: A. Storck, 1898. Pp. xii + 247.

——. "La Criminalité Ancillaire," *Archives d'Anthropologie Criminelle,* XXI (1906), 507-68, 677-96, 881-901.

——. *La Servante Criminelle.* Paris: A. Maloine, 1908. Pp. 459.

Sachs, Hanns. "The Wish to be a Man," *The International Journal of Psychoanalysis,* I (1920), 262-67.

Sanger, Margaret. *Happiness in Marriage.* New York: Blue Ribbon Books, 1926. Pp. 231.

Sauer, Wilhelm. *Kriminalsoziologie,* II. Berlin: Dr. Walther Rothschild, 1933. Pp. 181-629.

Scheinfeld, Amram. *Women and Men.* New York: Harcourt, Brace and Company, 1944. Pp. xx + 453.

Schmitz, Käte. *Die Kriminalität der Frau.* Bochum-Langendreer: Heinrich Pöppinghaus o.H.G., 1937. Pp. 74.

Schneickert, Hans. "Das Weib als Erpresserin und Anstifterin," *Abhandlungen aus dem Gebiete der Sexualforschung,* I (1918-19), 1-39.

Schröder, Hein. "Anlage und Umwelt in ihrer Bedeutung für die Verwahrlosung weiblicher Jugendlicher," *Allgemeine Zeitschrift für die Psychiatrie und ihre Grenzgebiete,* CXII-CXIII (1939), Supplement 12 (1939), pp. 224-36.

Scot, Reginald. *The discouerie of witchcraft.* London: 1584. Pp. 560.

Seagrave, Mabel. "Causes Underlying Sex Delinquency in Young Girls," *Journal of Social Hygiene,* XII (1926), 523-29.

Sellheim, Hugo. *Gemütsverstimmungen der Frau.* Stuttgart: Ferdinand Enke Verlag, 1930. Pp. 81.

Sellin, Thorsten. "The Basis of a Crime Index," *Journal of the American Institute of Criminal Law and Criminology,* XXII (1931-32), 335-56.

——. *Research Memorandum on Crime in the Depression.* New York: Social Science Research Council, 1937. Pp. viii + 133.

Sellin, Thorsten. *Culture Conflict and Crime.* New York: Social Science Research Council, 1938. Pp. x + 116.

———. *War and Crime: A Research Memorandum.* New York: Social Science Research Council, 1942. Pp. 24.

Seward, Georgene H. *Sex and the Social Order.* New York: McGraw-Hill Book Company, 1946. Pp. xii + 301.

Shalloo, J. P. *Private Police: With Special Reference to Pennsylvania.* Philadelphia: The American Academy of Political and Social Science, 1933. Pp. x + 224.

Sharpe, May Churchill. *Chicago May.* New York: The Macaulay Company, 1928. Pp. 336.

Shideler, Ernest H. "Family Disintegration and the Delinquent Boy in the United States," *Journal of the American Institute of Criminal Law and Criminology,* VIII (1917-18), 709-32.

Sighele, Scipio. *Le Crime A Deux,* trans. into French by Vincent Palmer from the second Italian ed. Lyon: A. Storck, 1893. Pp. viii + 284.

Skaggs, E. B. "Sex Differences in Moral Attitudes," *The Journal of Social Psychology,* XI (1940), 3-10.

Societé De Médecine Légale de France, Bulletin Officiel de la. "Rapport De La Commission Chargée D'Etudier Les Questions Concernant L'Avortement Et La Dénatalité" (B. Desplas, Rapporteur), *Annales de Médecine Légale,* XIX (1939), 538-44.

Söderman, Harry, and O'Connell, John J. *Modern Criminal Investigation.* New York: Funk & Wagnalls Company; 10th printing, 1941. Pp. xvi + 461.

Spaulding, Edith R. "The Results of Mental and Physical Examinations of Four Hundred Women Offenders—With Particular Reference to Their Treatment During Commitment," *Journal of the American Institute of Criminal Law and Criminology,* V (1914-15), 704-17.

———. "The Value of Mental, Physical and Social Studies of Delinquent Women," *Journal of the American Institute of Criminal Law and Criminology,* IX (1918-19), 80-97.

Stade, Reinhold. *Frauentypen aus dem Gefängnisleben.* Leipzig: Dörffling & Franke, 1903. Pp. 290.

Steidle, Hans. "Thallium, das neue Mord und Selbstmordgift," *Die Medizinische Welt,* XIII (1939), 1557-60.

Stekel, Wilhelm. "The Sexual Root of Kleptomania," *Journal of the American Institute of Criminal Law and Criminology,* II (1911-12), 239-46.

Sullenger, T. E. "Female Criminality in Omaha," *Journal of Criminal Law and Criminology,* XXVII (1936-37), 706-11.

Sutherland, Edwin H. *Principles of Criminology.* Philadelphia: J. B. Lippincott Company; 2nd ed., 1934. Pp. viii + 611.

———. *Principles of Criminology.* Philadelphia: J. B. Lippincott Company; 3rd ed., 1939. Pp. x + 651.

Taft, Donald Reed. *Criminology*. New York: The Macmillan Company, 1942. Pp. xii + 708.

Tarde, Gabriel. "La Criminalité Professionelle," Rapport présenté au Quatrième Congrès d'Anthropologie Criminelle, *Archives d'Anthropologie Criminelle*, XI (1896), 538-60.

Tarnowsky, Pauline. *Les Femmes Homicides*. Paris: Félix Alcan, 1908. Pp. viii + 591.

Taussig, Frederick J. *Abortion Spontaneous and Induced, Medical and Social Aspects*. St. Louis: The C. V. Mosby Company, 1936. Pp. 536.

Taylor, Alfred S. *Medical Jurisprudence*. Philadelphia: Lea and Blanchard, 1850. Pp. xvi + 670.

Teichmann, Hans Georg. *Meineidige und Meineidssituationen*. Leipzig: Ernst Wiegandt Verlagsbuchhandlung, 1935. Pp. 71.

Thomas, Dorothy Swaine. *Social Aspects of the Business Cycle*. New York: Alfred A. Knopf, 1927. Pp. xvi + 217.

Thomas, W. I. *The Unadjusted Girl*. Boston: Little, Brown, and Company, 1923. Pp. xviii + 261.

Thomas, William I., and Znaniecki, Florian. *The Polish Peasant in Europe and America*, I. Chicago: The University of Chicago Press, 1918. Pp. xii + 526.

Thompson, C. J. S. *Poisons and Poisoners*. London: Harold Shaylor, 1931. Pp. 392.

Thompson, Clara. "Cultural Pressures in the Psychology of Women," *Psychiatry*, V (1942), 331-39.

Thompson, Helen Bradford. *The Mental Traits of Sex*. Chicago: The University of Chicago Press, 1903. Pp. vii + 188.

Thorbecke, Clara. "Über jugendliche Kindesmörderinnen," *Archiv für Kriminologie*, LXXVII (1925), 51-58.

Ungar, E. "Der Nachweis des Kindesmordes," in *Gerichtsärztliche und Polizeiärztliche Technik, Ein Handbuch für Studierende, Ärzte, Medizinalbeamte und Juristen*. (Th. Lochte, ed.). Wiesbaden: J. F. Bergmann, 1914. Pp. 598-641.

Wadler, Arnold. *Die Verbrechensbewegung im östlichen Europa*, I, *(Die Kriminalität der Balkanländer)*. München: Hans Sachs Verlag, 1908. Pp. 263.

Warker, Ely van de, M.D. "The Relations of Women to Crime," I and II, *The Popular Science Monthly*, VIII (1875-76), (I); 1-16 and (II); 334-44.

Watkins, Raymond E. "A Five-Year Study of Abortion," *American Journal of Obstetrics and Gynecology*, XXVI (1933), 161-72.

Waugh, Benjamin. "Babyfarming," *The Contemporary Review*, LVII (1890), 700-14.

Webb, Mary Louise. "Delinquency in the Making," *Journal of Social Hygiene*, XXIX (1943), 502-10.

Weidensall, Jean. *The Mentality of the Criminal Woman*, Educational

Psychology Monographs No. 14. Baltimore: Warwick and York, Inc., 1916. Pp. xx + 332.

Weinberg, Siegfried. "Über den Einfluss der Geschlechtsfunktionen auf die weibliche Kriminalität," *Juristisch-psychiatrische Grenzfragen,* VI, Heft 1 (1907), pp. 1-34.

Weiss, Edward, and English, O. Spurgeon. *Psychosomatic Medicine.* Philadelphia: W. B. Saunders Co., 1943. Pp. xxiv + 687.

Wellman, Francis L. *The Art of Cross-Examination.* New York: The Macmillan Company, 1916. Pp. 404.

Werner, A. "Die Rolle des Schwachsinns in der Kriminalität," *Monatsschrift für Psychiatrie und Neurologie,* CX (1945), 1-46.

Willoughby, Raymond Royce. "The Relationship to Emotionality of Age, Sex and Conjugal Condition," *The American Journal of Sociology,* XLIII (1937-38), 920-31.

Wood, Arthur Evans, and Waite, John Barker. *Crime and its Treatment.* New York: American Book Company, 1941. Pp. x + 742.

Woolston, Howard B. *Prostitution in the United States,* I. New York: The Century Company, 1921. Pp. xvi + 360.

Work, Monroe N. (Ed.). *Negro Year Book 1931-32.* Tuskegee Institute, Alabama.

———. *Negro Year Book 1937-38.* Tuskegee Institute, Alabama.

Wulffen, Erich. *Das Weib als Sexualverbrecherin.* Berlin: Paul Langenscheidt, 1923. Pp. viii + 431.

Yarnell, Helen. "Fire Setting in Children," *The American Journal of Orthopsychiatry,* X (1940), 272-86.

Zeleny, Leslie Day. "Feeble-Mindedness and Criminal Conduct," *The American Journal of Sociology,* XXXVIII (1932-33), 564-76.

Zilboorg, Gregory. "Masculine and Feminine," *Psychiatry,* VII (1944), 257-96.

INDEX

22512

PB 3785